The CAMBRIDGESHIRE Cook Book

A celebration of the amazing food & drink on our doorstep.
Featuring over 40 stunning recipes.

FOREWORD

That moment we got our first star, well, it was like my world was complete…

See, when I first came to Cambridge, there'd never been a Michelin starred restaurant in the region.

Needless to say, I took immense pride in that. Not only was it a reward for all the hard work and belief we'd put into achieving it – but it also felt like I was giving something special back to the area I'd fallen in love with.

I'll always remember the day I started at Midsummer House. Michael Winner was booked in for dinner, my wife had just told me she was pregnant, and my business partner called me to say we had six months to make it work otherwise we'd have to close.

That was in 1998, I was 25, but I was fearless.

I'd trained and worked with some of the most incredible, passionate and utterly crazy chefs in the world – and I'd literally lived in the kitchen since leaving school. Seriously, I'd never even set foot in a pub until I was 24, and I'd missed every family event going.

But it was all leading here…

I look out of my window every day and it makes me truly happy. I honestly believe I've got the best restaurant in the country, in the best region in the country, surrounded by the best people and producers in the country.

Our food and drink scene is positively buzzing, and it's important we celebrate that, which is why I'm so thrilled to be a part of this.

Coming here was the best move I ever made – and I genuinely wouldn't want to cook anywhere else.

Once you've read this book, I'm sure you'll feel the same.

Enjoy.

Daniel Clifford – Midsummer House

CONTENTS

The Cambridgeshire Cook Book

First edition printed in 2015 in the UK.

ISBN: 978-0-9928981-9-9

Compiled by: Lisa Pullen

Written by: Carl Reid

Photography by: Tim Green
www.timgreenphotographer.co.uk

Edited by: Rachel Heward, Joshua Hackett

Designed by: Paul Cocker

Cover art: Lucy Rivers

Thank you: Daniel Clifford, Dale Pinnock, Jin Yee Chung, Gerla de Boer, Hayley Reynolds, Jane Fairclough

me:ze
PUBLISHING

Published by Meze Publishing Limited

Unit 1 Beehive Works

Milton Street

Sheffield S3 7WL

web: www.mezepublishing.co.uk

Tel: 0114 275 7709

email: info@mezepublishing.co.uk

Printed by Bell and Bain Ltd, Glasgow

Like lots of young girls, I got into baking from an early age. When I was about six or seven it would get to the weekend and I would be desperate to go 'round to my Nan's house where we would bake cakes and doughy cheese straws – she was a wicked cook! I always thought Sunday dinner at her house was like a big, medieval banquet. She would make really hearty, homemade food like oxtail casserole with dumplings or a roast with all the trimmings. We'd all crowd around the table, it was a huge free for all… and I would craftily sneak the dogs what I could under the table. As I got a bit older, my mum had a job as a school cook in the local secondary school and, contrary to popular belief, she can actually cook! Her specialty is a light, fresh-cream, Victoria sponge that we eat in the garden on the sunbeds whilst having a natter and catching some rays. Although I have to say, to this day she's still never made me her famous fudge tart – which I remind her of at least twice a year!

When it comes to cooking at home now, if it's fresh and takes less than 10 minutes to cook and prepare, then it's a winner for me. There are so many gorgeous places you can get locally produced, fresh ingredients that, I think, give food that extra bit of love, which is the most important ingredient when you are cooking. I love popping down to the Sunday farmers' market in my local town of St Neots, and every time I find it near impossible to not bring back a huge, homemade Scotch egg!

There is a great street food scene in Cambridge which has grown popular over the last few years. Regular food markets across the city are handy to visit and pick up a late lunch – something which I invariably do after shopping in the Grafton Centre and the Grand Arcade all morning. I also enjoy special foodie events at places like Gog Magog Hills and Burwash Manor, which are full of local foodies and wonderful local produce. I love going into Tom's cakes in St Ives where they have the most incredible chocolate and cherry macaroons to satisfy my sweet tooth, or if I am after a relaxing afternoon, I'll go to The Urban Shed where you can listen to vinyl and have a bite to eat.

It's been an absolute pleasure being involved in The Cambridgeshire Cook Book and it's further opened my eyes to how awesome my county really is when it comes to drinking and dining. I hope you get as much pleasure out of reading this as I had working on it…

Lisa Pullen - Meze Publishing

Welcome to CAMBRIDGE

It's not difficult to find delicious food in Cambridge if you look carefully – though many are tucked away in a small alleyway or away from the crowds… but it's well worth the search,

The food scene of Cambridge is positively booming with innovative restaurants popping up all the time, a vibrant street food scene and Michelin-starred restaurants in the city centre. We're very lucky to be spoilt for choice, the countryside of Cambridge has some interesting gems too.

When you think of Cambridge, you think famous colleges – they almost look as if they are made out of sugar in the bright sunlight. If you move away from King's Parade, and look behind this impressive facade, you'll find that one of the oldest university cities of England is 'peppered with international cuisine'.

Good food needs good wine – and there's plenty! Tread carefully on Kings Parade as some of the wine cellars run under the streets of Cambridge.

Looking to explore the city through the eyes of a foodie? Walk our walk of fame! Start at Fitzbillies for the stickiest buns in the world, head off to Aromi for Sicilian food to die for, tuck into some delicious Hungarian lángos on the market, get the low down on how to make the perfect fudge from Lee at the Fudge Kitchen, then the best cheese and handmade pies in town at The Cheese Company. Get your Scotch egg kick at The Free Press pub – and good old fish and chips from the Sea Tree at the back end of Mill Road. Make your way back into town to Adilia at the Norfolk Street bakery for her delicious Pastel del Nata and, to polish off the tour – delicious Gelato from Jack's Gelato at Nord.

Have we whet your appetite? Read on, and we're sure you'll keep coming back – as many have done before you.

Gerla de Boer – Cambridge Food Tour

Dale Pinnock's
CHICKEN STUFFED WITH SPINACH

and sun-dried tomatoes with a Mediterranean lentil stew. Serves 2.

Dale Pinnock, aka 'The Medicinal Chef', combines the science of nutritional medicine with the culinary arts.
An award-winning author of nine books, now published in 18 languages and available in over 20 countries. Dale has become a prominent spokesperson for healthy eating in the British media – being an authoritarian voice of evidence and science rather than fads and fashion. With many regular appearances on shows such as ITV's 'The Alan Titchmarsh Show, 'Lorraine' and 'This Morning', along with Ireland's 'Four Live', 'The Today Show', and 'Ireland AM', Dale is showcasing eating well in the real world. Delicious, fresh, wholesome, indulgent food, that explains what is good for you and why – without all the fluff and nonsense...

Ingredients

1 large red onion, finely chopped

2 cloves garlic, finely chopped

1 large courgette, sliced into half rounds

400g tin green lentils, drained

300g passata

2 skinless chicken breasts

2 large handfuls baby spinach leaves

4 large sun-dried tomatoes

4 rashers smoked bacon

Olive oil

Sea salt

Freshly ground black pepper

Method

Preheat the oven to 200°c.

Place the spinach into a sieve over a pan of boiling water and cover with a lid. Steam for 2 minutes maximum, just enough to wilt the leaves. Allow to cool and squeeze as much of the water out as possible.

Sauté the onion and garlic in a little olive oil, until the onion begins to soften.

At this stage, add in the sliced courgette and continue to sauté until the onion has softened completely and is turning transparent, and the courgette is beginning to soften.

Add the lentils and the passata and a generous pinch of sea salt and some cracked black pepper.

Simmer for about 15 minutes, stirring frequently until the passata has reduced and the flavours have intensified. It should be a very thick stew-like texture, rather than too wet.

Whilst the stew is simmering, cut a slice along the side of each of the chicken breasts, so as to make a pocket to fill.

Fill the pocket in the chicken with two sun-dried tomatoes each. Then add as much of the squeezed wilted spinach in as you can, pushing it into the pocket, but ensuring you don't push so hard it splits the breast.

Once the breast is stuffed, wrap two rashers of smoked bacon around each one to seal it up into a parcel. Place these on a tray and then bake in the oven for around 20-25 minutes.

Plate up by placing an island of the stew in the centre of the serving plate. Slice the chicken carefully and lay the slices on top of the stew.

Afternoon TEASE

First things first – Afternoon Tease don't do afternoon teas.
What they do though, is all things cake...

Based on King Street in Cambridge, Afternoon Tease is the brainchild of cake baker Jo Kruczynska, who worked towards opening the venture for seven years – blogging her baking adventures along the way.

A former illustrator, Jo packed in her 9-5 and set off travelling, garnering inspirations from cafés in Australia and New Zealand.

Offering a community café vibe, it's a cosy and welcoming establishment with daily specials and everything made freshly and enthusiastically on-site using local produce whenever possible.

Diners can enjoy indulgent treats such as chocolate Guinness cake with cream cheese icing, lemon drizzle cake with lemon curd buttercream icing or gooey chocolate cake with ganache icing with tasty gluten-free options available.

A champion of the independent scene, Afternoon Tease's cakes are so popular you can even find them outside of the shop in Cambridge's Duke House, Hot Numbers Coffee and Nanna Mexico.

In addition to the plethora of cakes, Afternoon Tease offers hearty brunches and lunches – with everything from homemade smoked chorizo jam, avocado and poached eggs on Dovecote Bakery sourdough toast for the former, to the 'Reuben Toastie' (pastrami, sauerkraut, gherkins, Swiss cheese and homemade Russian dressing on light rye) for the latter.

Something of a warm hug on a cold day, Afternoon Tease is comfort eating at its finest. Crazy about coffee, crackers for cakes, and passionate about produce – this is undoubtedly a café with a difference...

Afternoon Tease

Cheese scones (let us warm it for you) £3

MARKET BLEND
Espresso

Afternoon Tease
ORANGE DRIZZLE CAKE

With dark chocolate ganache icing.

Ingredients

For the cake:

350g egg yolks and whites (approximately 6-7 eggs)

350g unsalted butter, softened

350g caster sugar

350g plain flour

3½ tsp baking powder

2 large oranges, zest only

For the orange drizzle:

75g orange juice (use the oranges that you zested earlier)

75g caster sugar

For the dark chocolate ganache:

130g dark chocolate, chopped into small pieces

200ml double cream

1½ tbsp caster sugar

Method

Grease and line the bottom and sides of two 20cm cake tins.

Preheat the oven to 180°c (fan oven 160°c).

Using an electric mixer, cream the butter, sugar and orange zest together in a large mixing bowl until light and airy.

Add the eggs a few at a time, mixing after each addition until you have a thinner creamy mixture. If it curdles a little, don't panic!

You're now finished with the electric mixer, so make sure you remove any orange zest that may have got stuck around the beaters – you don't want to waste any.

Sift in the flour and baking powder and fold in using a spatula. Take your time, being careful not to beat all the air out of your mixture. When fully incorporated, divide the mixture between the cake tins.

Level each tin, neatening the edges so that the cake mixture is not spread up the sides. Finally, make a small indent in the centre of the cake – this ensures that the cakes level out as they cook instead of rising into large domes.

Bake in the oven for 25 minutes.

Combine the orange drizzle ingredients in a saucepan and heat until the sugar has dissolved then set aside.

To make the ganache, put the chocolate in a large bowl.

Heat the cream and sugar gently in a saucepan until just on the verge of boiling point.

Pour the cream over the chocolate and stir well until it has all melted and the ganache is smooth.

Leave to cool until the ganache has set to a spreadable consistency.

When you check the cake for the first time, do a 'wobble test'. If it wobbles when you shake it (gently), it needs another 5 minutes. Keep checking and, when it doesn't wobble, insert a skewer into the middle of the cakes – it should come out clean.

Prick both cakes all over with a skewer and spoon over the orange drizzle whilst the cakes are still warm and in their tins.

Once cooled, remove the cakes from the tins. Use half the ganache to sandwich them together and coat the top of the cake with the rest. If you're feeling confident, why not try swirling the top of the cake to look like a spiral?

Anchors AWAY

With a history that dates back to 1650, if only The Anchor's walls could talk...

Back in 1630, Dutch drainage engineer Cornelius Vermuyden was commissioned by the Earl of Bedford to drain the Fens for agricultural use. At this time, the area had become a haunt for the very worst of society.

The Anchor Inn was built around 1650, beside the bank of the New Bedford River (aka 'The Hundred Foot Drain'), to provide shelter for the workers who were mainly Scottish prisoners of war captured by Oliver Cromwell in a recent victory over the Scots. My, how times have changed…

Based in Sutton Gault (Gault's the name of the thick clay used to construct the river banks), The Anchor today has evolved to offer all mod-cons, whilst still retaining a timeless charm and antiquity.

The Anchor Inn offers a warm welcome, enhanced by a roaring log fire in the winter, and an intimate atmosphere. The menu serves up modern British cuisine with an emphasis on seasonal and traditional ingredients.

Local produce features heavily, such as Brancaster oysters, mussels, Bottisham smoked products, venison from the Denham Estate and hand-dressed crabs from Cromer, whilst many underused British ingredients such as oxtail, cod cheeks, and pigs' trotters are all creatively used by the talented kitchen team.

It's award-winning fare is also achieving recognition in all the major food guides including Good Food Guide, Good Pub Guide, Michelin Guide and Which Guide to Country Pubs, amongst others.

Fancy braised pork cheek with ham hock terrine, swede fondant, gooseberry ketchup, fennel and sage and white onion sauce? Perhaps a dark chocolate cigar filled with chocolate mousse with blackcurrant parfait and hibiscus marshmallow for your dessert?

Whatever you opt for, this is imaginative, quality food of the very highest order – all served with a large slice of history…

The Anchor Inn

DATES IN BACON

with mustard cream sauce.

This popular starter has been on our menu for at least 15 years
by demand of our regular customers.

Ingredients

12 rashers smoked streaky bacon

24 stoneless dates, such as Mejool

For the sauce:

Large knob unsalted butter

1 clove garlic, finely chopped

1 large shallot, finely chopped

150ml dry white wine

284ml carton whipping cream

2 heaped tsp grain mustard

Salt and freshly ground pepper

To garnish:

Chopped parsley (optional)

Method

Preheat the oven to 230°c.

Hold a rasher of bacon by one end and use the blunt side of a knife to gently stretch it out by about another quarter – this helps make the bacon crispier when cooked. Repeat with all the bacon. Cut each rasher in half and roll one half around each date. Refrigerate while you make the sauce.

Melt the butter in a frying pan over a gentle heat, add the garlic and shallot and sweat them gently for about 5 minutes until soft but not coloured. Add the wine, turn up the heat and boil until the liquid is reduced by a half. Strain the mixture through a sieve and return to the pan. Add the cream and mustard, bring to a rolling boil and boil for 30 seconds. Season if necessary (bear in mind that the bacon is quite salty).

Divide the mustard cream between four 10-12cm diameter gratin dishes. Add six dates to each dish. Bake for 8-10 minutes until the sauce is bubbling and the bacon browning. Finish off the dish with 2 minutes under a very hot grill to really crisp up the bacon.

That's AROMI

The beginnings of popular Cambridge eatery Aromi
is something of a love story...

Founders Francesco and Ofelia were childhood sweethearts, who arrived in Cambridge back in 2003 to study. Ultimately, the love birds then fell for the city itself, and decided to put down permanent roots. In 2013, Aromi was born – following the arrival of in-laws Salvatore and Alessandra Cipriani, who brought with them experience of running Caffe Cipriani in the beautiful baroque town of Acireale, Sicily – a venture originally set up by Salvatore's father Michele back in 1957.

As you can see, this is the real deal when it comes to authentic Italian cuisine, the original Aromi ethos of handcrafting honest products using traditional Sicilian techniques, and only the finest sourced Italian ingredients remains true today.

Based in the heart of Cambridge, Aromi is now a much loved and lauded independent café, serving up a modern day slice of Sicilian life – offering charm in abundance, stunning food, and that famously cheerful Mediterranean atmosphere.

From fantastic focaccia and flatbreads, to the perfect rustic pizza and an enticing selection of delicious bite-sized pasticceria, everything here is lovingly handcrafted.

Most of their products made up from their famous sourdough which is allowed to rest for three days to ensure that super light texture and beautifully bubbly crust. And all that's before we get to the stunning artisan gelato, homemade every day on the premises, using a much-loved family recipe.

Aromi means 'flavour' and, needless to say, this establishment lives up to its name. Big time. So, for all lovers of Italian food, head to Aromi – for Italian food, made with love...

Photo: Alessandra Spairani

Aromi
CARTOCCIATE CON SPINACI

Spinach Calzoni. Makes 9 cartocciate.
Super popular in Sicily, and sold in all the local cafés, this delicate dish is a family recipe – delicious when served warm with a fresh salad and a side of olives.

Ingredients

For the dough:

500g '00' grade flour

50g caster sugar

10g salt

10g instant yeast

50g unsalted butter, softened

300ml cool water

One egg, beaten

For the filling:

300g cooked baby spinach

300g mozzarella cheese, cut into 9 strips

9 tbsp tomato sauce (see below)

For the tomato sauce:

2 tbsp olive oil

1 clove garlic

2 basil leaves

1 tin plum tomatoes (400g)

Salt and pepper to season

Method

Using a mixer fitted with a dough hook, pour the flour into the mixing bowl.

Add the salt and sugar at one side and the yeast to the other side of the bowl.

Add the softened butter and three quarters of the water, then mix on a low speed. As the dough begins to come together, add the remaining water and mix for about 4 minutes – first on low speed and then for 1-2 minutes on a medium speed. The dough is ready when it feels smooth and silky.

Tip the dough onto a floured surface and divide into nine pieces, each weighing about 90g. Roll each piece into a smooth ball, rotating the ball quickly between your hand and the surface.

Place the rolls on three medium size pre-lined baking trays (three rolls per tray), brush the top with an oiled brush and allow them to rest for about 2 hours.

When the dough rolls are ready, flatten them with your hands to form oval shapes of about six inches long. Put two spoonfuls of spinach, a spoonful of tomato sauce and one strip of mozzarella cheese into the centre of each oval.

Lift the two longer ends of the dough and fold them up together to form a parcel, leaving the top and the bottom of the cartocciate open to reveal the ingredients.

Let these rest for an hour and preheat your oven to 180°c.

Brush the top of the cartocciate with the beaten egg and bake in the oven for about 15-20 minutes, or until golden.

For the tomato sauce

Gently heat two tablespoons of olive oil in a small pan and add one peeled clove of garlic. As this begins to colour, add a couple of basil leaves and a tin of plum tomatoes, about 400g. Squash the tomatoes down as much as you can with a wooden spoon, and then season with salt and pepper.

Lower the heat and cook for about 15-20 minutes, until the sauce reaches a nice rich consistency to spread on your cartocciate.

Brotherly LOVE...

With four generations of experience, the butchery business is in the blood of the Barker Bros.

When it comes to meat, it's fair to say Barker Bros Butchers know a thing or two…

With a history dating back to the 1900s, it's a true family business, with four generations plying their trade in the industry.

Owner Stuart started work in the shop at 14, taking over the reins from father David, who also took over from his father. With butchery in the blood though, retirement is proving tricky for David who simply cannot keep away from the booming business.

Selling a whopping variety of high quality meats, at incredibly competitive prices, all produce is sourced locally whenever possible, whilst a whole host of items are created in-house by the talented team – think home-cured bacon, their own hams and award-winning sausages.

In addition to the meat and game, Barker Bros also serve up fish, cheese, bread and eggs, along with a fine selection of deli produce – including their own delicious mackerel pâté.

Situated in Shelford, the shop has expanded due to demand over the years, ultimately becoming something of a pillar of the community, and with Stuart and wife Katy's young family of Jack, William and Daisy growing up fast, it would seem the Barker Bros story is set to continue for many years to come.

For well-informed friendly service, not to mention marvellous meats and more, keep it a family affair with Barker Bros.

Barker Bros Butchers

The BLACK STUFF

Sister pub to The Red Lion Hinxton, the beautiful Black Bull Inn has been a fixture in the heart of the historic village of Balsham since the 16th century.

Purchased by Alex Clarke in 2011, The Black Bull Inn in Balsham offered the perfect opportunity to set up another pub in a similar mould to The Red Lion – far enough away to reach a different market, but close enough to make the most of the advantages of a group.

Enjoying tranquil scenes outside thanks to a tree-lined sandstone dining patio at the front and a cosy south-facing beer garden at the back. Inside the cosy venue has enjoyed a sympathetic refurbishment making the most of its charming Grade II listed features.

A multi award-winner, The Black Bull offers an AA rosette menu featuring a seasonal mix of contemporary and traditional dishes, all cooked to order using primarily fresh local produce. Be it smoked mackerel with golden raisin purée and spiced bread for your starter, to slow-braised shin of beef with courgette and risotto Milanese for your main – it's very much a case of carefully selected dishes done absolutely brilliantly.

Then there's the famous Black Bull Pie – a signature steak and ale number, fully encased in short crust pastry with seasonal vegetables and gravy. The menus change every two months in addition to daily specials boards, seasonality plays a huge part in what they do here. The result is gastropub dining at its best.

Listed in industry bible The Good Pub Guide (which they achieved almost immediately after taking over), there are also five luxurious four star guest rooms available which have been completely refurbished to bring them up to The Red Lion standards.

Be it a pint and a bite, or the full gastro dining experience, grab the bull by the horns and head along…

See the recipe with sister pub, The Red Lion Hinxton on page 142.

Black Bull Inn

Blue is THE COLOUR

The beating heart of Hardwick, The Blue Lion's roar can be heard for miles.

A thriving hub for the Hardwick community, The Blue Lion has been trading as a pub since way back in 1737.

Owners Luke Edwards and Stuart Tuck have a wealth of experience in serving classic pub cuisine in and around Cambridge, they pride themselves on freshness, seasonality and the use of locally sourced products… as well as thinking outside the box.

The menu changes regularly and the specials board always offers up a treat or two – dishes such as corned beef hash (made with their own beef) alongside kooky offerings such as 'green eggs and ham' (pea panna cotta with pressed and fried ham hock and confit hen's egg) and 'the rabbit rabbit rabbit' – designed for a friend who's a huge Chas & Dave fan. It's fun stuff. What's more, most of the food is gluten free.

Be it a fireside drink, quick snack or full evening meal, this quaint 17th century establishment delivers by the bucket load – a quality gastropub offering charm in abundance.

As well as the varied high quality menu, and a fantastic range of wines and beers, The Blue Lion in Hardwick also organises regular events and themed evenings ranging from fêtes and comedy marquees in the summer, to bonfire nights, murder mystery evenings and everything in between. Plus, their massive beer garden is simply *the* place to be when the sun's shining.

An active member of the local community, The Blue Lion is undoubtedly a pub with colour…

WORLD HOP MEDLEY

GREENE KING

THE BLUE LION
.Hardwick

Friendly welcome

Restaurant

Garden

The Blue Lion
RABBIT, RABBIT, RABBIT

A great dinner party dish – as the preparation can be done a few hours in advance. Plus, it has a real wow factor when presented. Requires one farmed rabbit, ask your butcher to remove the legs, shoulders and the loins. The bones can be roasted and used to make stock. Serves 2.

Ingredients

For the rabbit 'wellingtons':

2 rabbit loins

2 slices white bread

2 slices Parma ham

2 sprigs sage

10g butter, melted

For the rabbit croquette:

2 rabbit shoulders

The rest of the loaf of sliced white bread roughly torn into pieces

½ litre full-fat milk

1 onion, peeled and quartered

1 fresh bay leaf

1 tsp peppercorns

½ tsp ground mace

1 tsp salt

15g butter

1 tsp nutmeg

100g panko breadcrumbs

2 eggs

100g plain flour

300g duck fat

2 sprigs thyme

For the rabbit cottage pie:

2 rabbit legs

500ml cider

1 onion, finely diced

1 carrot finely diced

1 stick celery finely diced

1 leek finely sliced

2 sprigs rosemary

200ml rabbit stock

500g Maris Piper potatoes, boiled in salted water and mashed with a little salt only

1 tbsp grain mustard

250g black pudding

2 baby carrots, cooked for 3–4 mins in boiling water and cooled in iced water

Method

Place the rabbit shoulders and legs into a roasting dish and cover with duck fat. Add the thyme and peppercorns, cover with foil and cook on the middle shelf of your oven at 180°c for 60-70 minutes. The meat should fall away from the bone once cooked.

Dice up the black pudding and whiz into very small pieces in a food processor. Place on a baking tray and leave on the bottom shelf of the oven until crispy. This should take 20-30 minutes. Remove from the oven and allow to cool.

Whilst the shoulders, legs and black pudding are cooking, you can make the bread sauce which will become the base for your croquettes.

Bring the milk, onion, bay leaves, mace, butter and nutmeg to a simmer and add the torn up bread to soak up the milk and go very thick. Take off the heat and add the salt. Put to one side to cool.

Once the rabbit is cooked, carefully remove it from the oil and allow to cool enough so you can remove the meat from the bones – keeping the shoulder and leg meat separate.

Mix the shoulder meat with the bread sauce mixture. Using a piece of cling film, roll the mix into a sausage shape as tight as possible. Tie the ends and place in the freezer for 30 minutes until firm enough to slice.

For the cottage pie, sweat the onion, carrot, celery and leek in a little oil until soft but not coloured, add the rosemary leaves, rabbit leg meat, cider and stock, bring to a simmer and cook until the liquor has reduced to approximately half. Add salt and pepper to taste.

Divide the cottage pie mix into two small single serving pie dishes or ramekins and allow to cool.

Once the pies have cooled, mix the grain mustard with the mashed potato and pipe or spread on top. Place in fridge until ready to serve.

Remove the croquette mixture from the freezer and slice into two equal pieces, beat the two eggs in a bowl. Remove the cling film and dip the croquettes into the flour then the egg and finely into the panko breadcrumbs – making sure they are completely covered. Place in fridge until ready to serve.

To make the 'wellingtons', remove the crusts from the two slices of bread, then using a rolling pin roll the bread slices as thin as you can. Place each flattened slice of bread on to a piece of cling film roughly twice the size of the bread. Brush each slice of bread with melted butter then lay a slice of Parma ham running the length of the bread. In the centre, lay two sage leaves and season with a little salt and pepper. Place one rabbit loin on to the sage leaves and season again. Starting at the edge closest to you, roll the bread over the rabbit loin until it forms a sausage shape. Keeping it as tight as possible, use the cling film to wrap the loin which will help keep its shape when you come to cook it. Leave in the fridge for at least two hours.

To serve, place your cottage pies in a 180°c oven for 15 minutes. Unwrap your 'wellingtons', brush with melted butter and place on a baking tray.

Over a medium heat, add 100ml vegetable oil to a deep sided frying pan. Once the oil is hot, add your croquettes and colour on all sides, this should take 3-4 minutes. Once golden brown, remove from the pan and place on the tray with the 'wellingtons'. Remove the pies from the oven and sprinkle the top with the black pudding crumb. Put back in the oven with the croquettes and 'wellingtons' for another 8 minutes. The rabbit 'wellingtons' should be just firm to the touch with a crisp toast exterior.

Once cooked, remove the pies and push a pre-blanched baby carrot into the top of each one with just the tip showing, Arrange on the plate with a croquette and 'wellington'.

At the restaurant, we serve this with a potato terrine, carrot purée and rabbit jus, but it also works with a creamy mashed potato or simply boiled potatoes tossed in a little butter and parsley. You can use whatever seasonal vegetables you prefer as a garnish and, if you don't have the rabbit stock, a good quality shop bought brown chicken stock reduced by half with a spoonful of apple sauce stirred through it works very nicely too.

Juniper ASCENDING

The Cambridge Distillery is a gin lover's dream – with Will and Lucy Lowe
the sandman and sandwoman behind it…

Husband and wife team Will and Lucy Lowe are the driving force behind this booming, boozy business, each bringing their own particular skills to the quintessentially British party.

Will is the Master Distiller whose career in the drinks industry is extensive. A Wine and Spirit Educator to professionals in the industry, he was awarded the title of International Wine and Spirits Championship Associate Judge of the Year, and is the winner of the highly coveted Wines from Spain scholarship for the Master of Wine qualification.

Lucy's background is in marketing and event management, which perfectly complements Will's technical skills. It was her passion for gin, glorious gin, which was in no small part the inspiration for The Cambridge Distillery.

Then there's arguably the most important member of the team, brand ambassador Darcy, the couple's pet Labrador whose walks in the fields of Cambridgeshire inspired their sensational seasonal blend.

They're also the world's first Gin Tailor – producing bespoke gin blends for individuals, institutions and some of the world's leading restaurants. Currently the U.K's smallest distillery, their uniquely small batch distillation allows them to tailor your gin to your exact specification.

The Cambridge Distillery was the first to create a truly seasonal gin, using only home grown and freshly foraged botanicals each season to create two distinct gins each year.

A victim of their own success, Cambridge Seasonal Gins often sell out within days, leaving a rather long gap until the next batch comes along. To solve this problem, they've released Cambridge Dry Gin – using local botanicals from all four seasons and available all year round.

A joint venture with experimental Copenhagen-based Nordic Food Lab gave birth to something rather special in the form of Anty Gin. Derived from the formic acid and pheromones of the red wood ant, each bottle contains the essence of approximately sixty-two wood ants and comes complete with a 50ml bottle of pure wood ant distillate.

Add to this The Cambridge Distillery's multi award-winning 'Japanese Gin', the first in the world to combine quintessential juniper notes with traditional Japanese botanicals, and you have a company that's really going places…

Cambridge Distillery
BASIL SMASH

Our favourite way to enjoy Cambridge Dry Gin is in a Basil Smash. It's simple enough to make and fantastically refreshing. Serves one.

Ingredients

6 fresh basil leaves

½ lemon

20ml sugar syrup

60ml Cambridge Dry Gin

Crushed and cubed ice

Method

Drop five of the basil leaves, juice from half a lemon, and sugar syrup into a cocktail shaker, then shake it vigorously with cubed ice.

Add the gin, then shake it all together.

Strain into a hi-ball glass filled with crushed ice, garnish with the remaining basil leaf, and enjoy!

Cambridge Distillery
TOKYO HIGH TEA

Our international award-winning Japanese Gin makes for a great afternoon or apértif cocktail. Serves one.

Ingredients

¼ cucumber

½ lemon

20ml sugar syrup

50ml Japanese Gin

1 red apple

Ice

Method

Muddle together the cucumber, juice of half a lemon and sugar syrup.

Pour in 50ml of Japanese Gin, add ice, then shake it all together.

Strain the cocktail into a martini glass and garnish with a couple of thin slices of apple on the glass.

Walk THE WALK

Think you know Cambridge? Think again – Cambridge Food Tour offers up the chance for you to experience the city anew through the eyes of a foodie...

Adopted Cambridge resident Gerla de Boer travelled and worked around the world, indulging in her passion for different cuisines, before settling in the city and ultimately setting up the now renowned Cambridge Food Tour.

Born in the Netherlands, Gerla's love affair with food and travel started at a young age then became more than just a hobby. With a professional background in the travel, hotel and hospitality industries also with experience in food development – and setting up a local Farmers' Market – it's fair to say Gerla knows a thing or three about filling your belly with quality, varied fare.

A foodie through and through, she still explores Cambridge as a tourist, with wide-eyed wonder constantly seeking out new culinary adventures.

A few hours under Gerla's guidance offers up far more than simply fabulous food and drink. It's an education about the city itself which will leave you feeling a true bond with your environment.

From wall scrawlings and ghost stories in The Eagle pub to the story of the statue of local legend Snowy Farr, right through to the Swan Ball at King's College (the only college allowed to eat swan) – it's as much a meal for the mind as it is the body.

There's an amazing world out there, right on the doorstep, meaning the tour is as much an experience for residents as it is for visitors.

During the tour you can look forward to meeting the locals and hearing their personal stories while enjoying some very tasty food and drink.

There are various options available. Scheduled tours include a seasonal selection of passionate foodie traders ranging from well-known places, street food vendors and hidden gems.

The 'four hour lunch' with the Cambridge Food Tour runs six days a week and includes at least 12 food tastings and a beer tasting. A 'four hour classic' Cambridge Food Tour runs on dedicated dates and includes at least 12 food tastings, an English cheese and tipples pairing and a beer tasting with tutoring. Finally the 'three hour pub tour' runs once a week with five food tastings with wine or beer.

Gerla and her fellow local foodies like to keep the tours intimate, between 4-14 people, for that personal touch that enables visitors and residents alike to look at the city in a whole new light.

Expect to experience everything from brilliant biscuits and fabulous fudge, to perfect pies, chips, chocolate and a whole lot more to boot. Oh, and needless to say, there'll be some delicious drink thrown in for good measure.

Highly rated on TripAdvisor, a Cambridge Food Tour promises to leave you hungry for more.

So, strap on your walking shoes, loosen your belt, and join the Cambridge Food Tour for some genuine food for thought…

AROMI
Cucina Siciliana dal 1957

School of THOUGHT

Can't cook? Won't cook?
A visit to the Cambridge Cookery School will change your perspective...

Founded in 2008 by Tine Roche and joined by business partner Liz Young in 2012, the Cambridge Cookery School is to cooking as Hogwarts is to witchcraft and wizardry.

A thoroughly hands-on experience, a variety of inspiring and fun classes await for every age and ability from team building exercises right through to hen parties and beyond. What's more, they all include a welcome drink, full meal (with wine), a recipe pack, apron, equipment and ingredients – they've thought of the lot.

An award-winning operation, 2013 saw 'Looking to Cook' naming them the 'Best Cookery School in UK and Ireland' – whilst 2014 saw the passionate lot shortlisted for the same title by Food and Travel magazine.

Featuring a team of talented and friendly chefs who garner great pleasure in teaching you the tricks of the trade, Cambridge Cookery School also dishes up plenty outside of its walls. With regular culinary trips and cooking holidays (listed by The Times as 'among the six best in Europe') on offer – think truffle hunting in Italy, to baking in wood fired ovens in Stockholm.

2015 ushered in big changes for the venture with the expansion of the cookery school and the long-awaited addition of a bakery, deli and café at the Homerton Business Centre. A natural evolution for the ambitious team, it offers one of the first kitchens in the country to be full kitted out with the latest Neff appliances – with controls that swipe like an iPad. The future is now.

A brilliant business that's clearly going places, this is one school that's a class above…

Cambridge Cookery School
FRESH ASPARAGUS

with nectarine, avocado and crab salad. Serves 4.

Ingredients

For the salad:

100g fresh asparagus

1 perfectly ripe avocado

8 radishes

2 nectarines

10 fresh mint leaves, cut into thin shreds

Fresh coriander leaves

100g picked white crab

For the dressing:

1 tbsp miso paste

1 tbsp rice vinegar

1 tsp tamari (wheat free soy sauce)

2 large tbsp natural yoghurt

Juice from 1 fresh lime

Salt and pepper

Method

Prepare the asparagus by removing the woody part of the stems. This is easily done by bending the base – it will snap in the right place.

Lightly roast the asparagus spears in a hot pan or on a griddle. Season with a little salt and pepper. Once cooked, place on kitchen towel.

Halve the avocado and scoop out the stone by using either your thumb or a spoon. Cut into quarters and slice each quarter thinly.

Thinly slice the four radishes and cut the remaining four in half. It's nice to keep the little green stalk for this – provided they're clean.

Cut the nectarines in half and remove the stone (similar process to the avocado), slice into thin wedges.

Take ten mint leaves and slice thinly. Pick the coriander leaves.

Before putting the salad together, mix all the dressing ingredients in a bowl and check the seasoning.

To assemble the salad, lay slices of avocado over the base of the plate, follow this with three quarters of the radish. Next, add the spears of asparagus and thin nectarine wedges. Using a teaspoon, evenly place spoonfuls of crab over the salad base. Scatter the remaining radish slices over the top, add salt and pepper, then drizzle over the dressing.

Scatter over the coriander and mint.

One big
HAPPY FAMILY

With five quality restaurants, and an ever expanding event dining operation, Cambscuisine is a major player on the Cambridge food scene...

A genuine local success story, Cambscuisine was founded in 2001 with the purchase of The Cock in the quintessentially British village of Hemingford Grey.

National Pub of the Year in the Good Pub Guide (2013), and Cambridgeshire Dining Pub of the Year (2015), it's safe to say they've turned the once 'smoky local boozer' into a much-loved pub and restaurant serving up fresh, seasonal fare with friendly, courteous service.

Also in the company's armoury are two 'chop houses' delivering no-nonsense British tucker. Firstly, The Cambridge Chop House, which lies just 50 yards from King's College Chapel in the heart of the city centre.

An unpretentious hangout, as you'd expect, the steaks are the stars of the show – but they'll also often feature more unusual meats such as squirrel and rook. They're big on real ale here, and the restaurant itself offers a fantastic cellar area with the ground floor boasting views of King's College Chapel and King's Parade.

St. John's Chop House on Northampton Street offers a more rustic dining setting housed in a 17th century brick building featuring naturally aged beams and wood burning stoves.

The restaurant is similar in ethos to its sister establishment, but with cosy private dining rooms upstairs it has earned a strong reputation for hosting larger groups.

The Tickell Arms, nestled in the quaint village of Whittlesford, offers a picturesque setting to enjoy a proper local pint and modern British cuisine which changes with the seasons. Real fires in the winter and a delightful garden room and terrace in the summer, have made this a real winner with locals.

The latest string to their bow is Smokeworks which, as the name suggests, serves up slow cooked barbecue food. Ribs and other meat cuts are brined, smoked, pulled and seasoned before pairing with beer, bourbon and milkshakes.

Lest we forget, Cambscuisine also operate the Cambridge Dining Company, your go-to business for high quality catering solutions, event management, restaurant quality food and service for your party.

They're a busy lot, but they certainly won't be resting on their laurels – so keep your eyes peeled for the next exciting instalment...

Cambscuisine
DUCK PARCEL

with sweet and sour cucumber. Serves 4 (as a starter).

Ingredients

For the duck parcels:

2 duck legs (each around 200–250g)

250g duck fat

1 red chilli

2 large spring onions

100g hoisin sauce

50g butter, melted

4 sheets filo pastry

Salt and pepper

For the cucumber garnish:

60ml white wine vinegar

125ml white wine

60g caster sugar

½ cucumber

½ red chilli

¼ red pepper

2 spring onions

8 mint leaves

Method

To confit the duck

If you have time, remove the duck legs from their packaging, season with salt and pepper, place in the loaf tin and rest overnight in the fridge covered in cling film.

Preheat oven to 150°c (130°c fan).

Melt the duck fat in a pan and pour over the duck legs in the loaf tin. The legs should be completely covered.

Cover with a layer of greaseproof paper and then with a layer of foil, tucking the foil tightly around the edge of the tin to stop any steam from escaping.

Cook in the centre of the oven for 3 hours or until the meat is tender and easily falls off the bone.

Carefully remove the duck legs from the hot fat using tongs and place on a sheet of greaseproof paper. Leave to cool.

Discard the skin and pull all the meat off the leg bones, placing it in a small mixing bowl. Cover in cling film and refrigerate for 30 minutes.

Meanwhile, deseed and finely slice the red chilli, then finely slice the spring onions.

Mix together the duck meat, red chilli, spring onion and hoisin sauce.

To assemble the duck parcel

Pre-heat the oven to 200°c (180°c fan).

Melt the butter in a small pan.

Lay out a sheet of filo pastry. Using a pastry brush, brush half the sheet with melted butter and fold it in half so that the buttered side sticks to the dry side. Repeat with the other 3 sheets.

Place the ring mould in the centre of the folded pastry and spoon in ¼ of the duck mixture.

Brush some more butter about 1cm in from the edge of the pastry in a ring around your meat mixture.

Carefully pick up the four corners of your pastry and bring together over your duck mix, pinch them all together and push down gently so the finished article looks like a money purse.

Repeat for all of the parcels, place on greaseproof paper, covered in the fridge until you are ready to use them (they will keep for 1-2 days in the fridge.)

Brush the outsides of the parcels with melted butter and cook in the centre of the oven for 15-20 minutes or until the pastry is golden and crisp.

To make the cucumber garnish

In a small pan, bring the white wine vinegar, white wine and sugar to the boil. Set aside to cool whilst preparing the other ingredients.

Peel the cucumber with a potato peeler into a bowl. Stop when you reach the seeds.

Finely slice the red chilli, red pepper, spring onions and mint leaves. Add to the cucumber.

Pour over the warm vinegar mix, cover in cling film and leave to steep for 30 minutes in the fridge, stirring occasionally.

To serve

Strain the cucumber garnish.

Place one hot duck parcel on a plate and garnish with a little sweet and sour cucumber.

French KISS

Rick and Heather Hurley are the couple to thank for bringing some French joie de vivre to Great Wilbraham...

Situated within the scenic surroundings of Great Wilbraham, The Carpenters Arms is a Great British boozer offering a healthy dose of French va-va-voom.

With a history dating back to 1640 (it's been a pub since 1729), traditional beams and classic décor greet you as you step into the cosy establishment which is operated by Rick and Heather Hurley. They took over the reins in 2009 and swiftly transformed it into a quality gastropub dishing up authentic French cuisine alongside British pub favourites.

The pair have plenty of previous experience, having ran the award-winning La Casa de la Nine restaurant in the South of France, while Heather herself has over 30 years experience as a chef.

The Carpenters also has its own on-site micro-brewery in the form of 'Crafty Beers' (you'll always find two of their own on tap at any one time), whilst wine inevitably plays a big part with many coming from family run vineyards in France where Rick and Heather know the owners personally.

Needless to say, the food here is next level, with daily specials written on blackboards to allow the couple to take advantage of the fresh, local produce arriving each day. Some of the dishes even include the tomatoes Heather grows in her greenhouse along with a wide selection of herbs.

The venue itself holds a five star elite rating for 'Scores on the Doors' (the number one national food hygiene rating scheme and the highest level achievable) and they have even won the 'Loo of the Year' award for 2015!

From smoked salmon, prawn and Champagne roulade with baby leaves, to roast guinea fowl suprême with straw potatoes, asparagus, carrot purée and walnut sauce, this is prestige pub dining – with all food produced in their own kitchen from fresh, raw ingredients.

Oh, and if you happen to hear mysterious footsteps upon your visit, don't worry … it's just the house ghost!

The Carpenters Arms

SCALLOPS

With puy lentils and a tomato and mixed herb sauce. Serves 4.

Ingredients

12 scallops

7 tbsp olive oil

4 large garlic cloves, crushed

4 chopped tomatoes (you can skin them but we like to leave the skins on to add some texture. Alternatively you could use a 400g tin of chopped tomatoes)

1 large pinch of mixed herbs, e.g. herbes de provence

2 tbsp red wine vinegar

1 tsp caster sugar

1 tbsp lemon juice

Chopped fresh herbs of your choice, we like basil but oregano, parsley or thyme would work as well

100g puy lentils

Olive oil

Salt and pepper, for seasoning

Method

Put the oil, garlic, tomatoes and mixed herbs into a pan. Bring to the boil on a medium heat then lower the heat and reduce the mixture until thick, stirring from time to time. Beware – it does spit as it thickens.

Put the vinegar and sugar into a small pan and boil to reduce down to about two teaspoons. Stir this into the tomato mixture and leave to cool slightly. Just before serving stir the fresh herbs and lemon juice into the sauce. Keep warm.

For the lentils, bring a large pan of well-salted water to the boil. Add the lentils and cook for 15-20 minutes. Drain well then return to the pan with a splash of olive oil and some salt and pepper to taste. Cover and keep warm.

For the scallops, heat a frying pan until it is very hot. Add one tablespoon of oil and sear the scallops for about 2 minutes on each side.

To serve, place three heaped spoons of lentils on each plate. Top these with scallops and then add the tomato sauce to the plate decoratively. Garnish with some sliced lemon or lime and some parsley.

Serve with some crusty bread alongside to mop up all those lovely juices!

The Carpenters Arms
SABLES BRETON

Ingredients

225g plain flour

Pinch of salt

1 tbsp baking powder

160g butter, softened

160g caster sugar

4 egg yolks

Method

Sift the flour, salt and baking powder together into a bowl.

Separately, cream the butter and sugar together until fluffy. Add the egg yolks, one at a time, beating well after each addition.

Fold the dry ingredients into the mixture carefully, taking care not to overwork it. Take a rectangle of cling film and lay it out on a work surface, place the mixture, which should be doughy, into the middle of the cling film and roll it all up into a cylinder shape. It should be approximately 8cm in diameter.

Place in the fridge to chill for 1 hour, after which time it should be firm and fairly solid. Cut into eight equal slices and place on a parchment lined tin. Bake at 180°c for 12-15 minutes, or until golden.

Remove from oven and allow to cool completely before filling.

We like to bake ours in mousse rings but egg rings would work, or in a large four hole Yorkshire pudding tin. You can bake them on the tray but they will spread and will not be so attractive.

Once they are cold, place a few pieces of your chosen fruit in each one, top with whipped cream and more fruit.

Serving suggestions

Strawberries, strawberry coulis, whipped cream with a few drops of vanilla extract mixed in and vanilla ice cream.

Raspberries, vanilla cream, as above, chocolate sauce and either vanilla or chocolate ice cream.

Rhubarb also works well with an orange sauce and vanilla or ginger ice cream.

For fruit coulis, blitz fruit in a food processor and add 1-2 tablespoons of icing sugar, blitz again then strain through a sieve to remove pips. Chill, then use to decorate your sables.

Say CHEESE!

Cheese+ is certainly one company that does exactly what its name suggests.

Cheese+ *loves* cheese.

Since the 1980s, Cheese+ have been serving up artisan cheese to delicatessens and fine dining establishments all over Cambridge delivering outstanding quality and with service levels that are simply second to none.

Your happiness is their number one priority and it's fair to say when working with them you'll be wearing your cheesiest grin!

A wealth of expertise lies at the heart of this family business, with the dedicated team going above and beyond to make your Cheese+ experience a rewarding and thoroughly enjoyable affair.

Lovingly ageing their cheeses so you can enjoy them at the very peak of perfection, you can expect brilliant blues like 'Bassingfield' and 'Blue Murder'.

In contrast, remarkable hard cheeses like the thirty two month matured 'Comte Reserve' exemplify a huge variety that will leave you feeling like a kid in a candy store.

Cheese+ also produce their own exclusive 'Duke' and 'Duchess' cheeses, inspired by Their Royal Highnesses, The Duke and Duchess of Cambridge. These unique artisan cheeses are fit for royalty.

Handmade using fresh morning milk which is rich in butterfat, 'The Duke' has a rich golden interior with dashes of royal blue. 'The Duchess' is bathed in Sparkling Rosé from Chilford Hall to create a cheese with an elegant curtsy of sweet notes.

Suffice to say, this is just the tip of the iceberg. As the name suggests, there is much more to these food-loving experts than just mountains of cheese.

Working closely with suppliers both locally and from across the globe to remain at the forefront of what's new, they've sourced a wonderful selection of everything you'd expect to find in your favourite deli. Think British, Italian and Spanish charcuterie. Olives, chutneys, oils, vinegars and much more besides…

Don't just say cheese – say Cheese+.

Cheese+

Cheese+ BAKED CHEESE

Baked cheese... Are you doing it right?

Ingredients

For the cheese:

250g Winslade or any recommended cheese for baking from your local deli

For the bread:

Crusty bread

1 sprig fresh rosemary

Extra virgin olive oil

For the fruit and nut side:

2 handfuls mixed nuts, finely chopped

2 handfuls dried cranberries, finely chopped

1 apple, finely chopped

1 small handful grapes, finely chopped

Honey, for drizzling

Pinch sea salt, for seasoning

Method

Let's be honest, baked Camembert is one of life's simple pleasures. It's a perfect dish for small dinner parties or a light lunch. However, many people often do it wrong. We love fine artisan cheeses and we don't like ruining them by shoving cloves of garlic, bits of woody rosemary or glugging white wine all over them (keep the wine for yourself!) All you have to do is get down to your local delicatessen and ask. 'What cheese do you stock which is ideal for baking?' You'll be surprised at what's on offer. From the subtleties of a Winslade, to the smelly washed rind of a Golden Cenarth (for those who are a little braver), the taste is all about the cheese!

You need to ascertain if the cheese is ripe enough for you. Too young and the flavour may underwhelm you. Too strong and it may knock you out. There's a bit of skill in this so do speak to whoever is on the deli counter for their opinion. Give it a big sniff and if under ripe, leave it at room temperature for about 3-4 hours to bring the flavours out a little bit. We've chosen Winslade from Stacey at Hampshire Cheese. It's the English Vacherin Mont d'Or, which we brought on for about 5 hours at room temperature (we like it strong).

Preheat the oven to 180°c. Do not remove the rind as it holds loads of flavour. Score the top and leave the cheese in its box with the lid off. Bake in the oven for 15-20 minutes. Give it a prod with a knife to check if it's at optimum gooeyness!

Tear your crusty bread into bite sized pieces and chuck them into a roasting tray. Now strip the sprig of rosemary and sprinkle the leaves on top of the bread. Drizzle with a little olive oil and add a tiny pinch of sea salt. Shake the tray and place it in the oven to cook with the cheese for a few minutes. Check back intermittently and shake the bread again for all round crispiness.

Put the nuts, cranberries, apple and grapes in a bowl. Drizzle with honey, add a pinch of salt and give it a loose stir.

When your bread is crisp and golden and your cheese is as oozy as can be, place everything on a board and devour!

Now reflect… this is how the cheesemaker intended the cheese to taste.

Game ON...

Creative cuisine, and a cosy, comforting welcome awaits
at Orwell's gorgeous Chequers gastropub.

With its roaring open fires and a family friendly ethos, The Chequers has swiftly established itself as a drinking and dining destination of note under the care and skill of husband and wife team David and Tina Cheng.

Based in Orwell, a mere eight miles from Cambridge and but a stone's throw from Wimpole Hall and Farm, it offers a relaxed and attractive destination for those seeking high-end cuisine without the added pretension.

David himself heads up the kitchen – a talented and charismatic chef who trained at the famous Cordon Bleu London and worked with celebrity chef Jun Tanaka before moving Cambridge way to work specifically in fine dining at Downing College in 2010.

Passionate about food, here it's all about offering amazing dishes that look as good as they taste, all the while keeping them at prices which everyday people can afford.

For David, it's simply a case of wanting to bring all his experience to the wider public's plate.

Utilising only the freshest, local ingredients available, it's hearty yet arty cuisine, with dishes such as the squid ragout with chorizo and crusty bread to start, right through to the trio of lamb with couscous, green olive tapenade, red pepper and sun blushed tomatoes for the main event. It's all of the very highest standard – as is the immaculately kept beer.

The young, dynamic team at The Chequers are always experimenting and looking to raise the bar. So, for affordable fine food, delivered with a down-to-earth attitude, get your game on at The Chequers.

The Chequers
DUO OF DUCK

With fondant potato, almond purée, broccoli and rhubarb. Serves 4.

Ingredients

1 whole duck (with giblets)

1.2kg duck fat

4 sprigs thyme

3 cloves garlic

2 shallots

2 large potatoes

100g blanched almonds

100ml milk

1 head broccoli

1 onion

2 carrots

1 leek

3 sticks celery

50g tomato purée

200ml red wine

2 sticks rhubarb

50ml grenadine

½cm ginger

150g sugar

Salt and pepper, for seasoning

Method

Take the breasts and legs off the duck carcass and score the skin of the breast. Roast the carcass and giblets for an hour at 195°c. In the meantime, colour off the onion, carrots, leek and celery in a large pan. When the carcass is roasted, add this to the pan with the tomato purée and cover with water. Simmer for four hours, topping up as necessary.

Melt 1kg of the duck fat. Peel the shallots and garlic and put in the base of an ovenproof dish with the thyme. Season the duck legs and place in the dish skin side up, then cover with the duck fat. Cover the dish and cook in a low oven at 145°c for an hour and a half.

Very lightly toast the almonds in a small dry pan then add the milk and a little salt and gently simmer for a couple of minutes. Liquidize the almonds and milk, adding more liquid if required.

Peel and trim the potatoes into 4-5cm thick discs. In a frying pan melt the rest of the duck fat and lightly colour the potatoes. Add a ladle of stock to the pan and simmer until only the fat remains, repeat this process until the potato is cooked.

In a pan melt the sugar with some water, the grenadine and the sliced ginger to make a syrup to poach the rhubarb. Prepare the rhubarb into 8cm pieces, then with a peeler or mandoline strip it up. Add to the boiling syrup then immediately remove from the heat to let the rhubarb cook in the residual heat.

Strain and reduce the stock with the red wine until it reaches sauce consistency.

When the duck legs have cooled enough to handle, remove from the fat and pick the meat off, removing the skin. Blend a third of the meat with the shallots and garlic add this back to the picked meat. Check the seasoning and form into cylinders using cling film. Add more fat if the mix doesn't hold. Refrigerate.

Have a pan of boiling water on to cook the broccoli. In a hot frying pan seal the breast, skin side first. Transfer to the oven at 195°c with the potato and cylinder. It will take about 8 minutes. While that's cooking blanch the broccoli, reheat the sauce, strips and purée. Assemble the elements on a plate and serve.

You Should COCOA...

Not only Cambridge's favourite chocolate shop –
but purveyors of delicious ice cream and hot chocolate too...

Since opening in 2009, Chocolat Chocolat's chocolatier Isabelle Chappell has had one goal in mind – to bring chocolate happiness to Cambridge.

Judging by the number of times the shop on St. Andrew's Street has been described by visitors as a 'little slice of chocolate heaven', it would seem she's succeeded...

Chocolat Chocolat has consistently been voted Cambridge's favourite chocolate shop – a reflection of the wide range of stunning handmade chocolate that can be found inside its wondrous walls.

But it's not just chocolate here. In the winter months you can treat yourself to a luxury hot chocolate to take away and, in the summer months, you can enjoy a refreshing handmade ice cream from their range of delicious flavours.

As a qualified Chocolatier, Isabelle (trained in France and Belgium) always believes in using only the best ingredients when it comes to creating Chocolat Chocolat's handmade

chocolate, such as their sheet chocolate bouquets and custom-made bars. She regularly creates new and exciting seasonal recipes which can often become a customer's new favourite.

Watching the chocolatiers make chocolate in the shop's kitchen proved so popular that, in 2010, Isabelle created a range of unique chocolate making and tasting courses, which are not only helping Cambridge chocolate lovers learn more about chocolate, but are also attracting visitors from far and wide.

Inspired by Isabelle's favourite Parisian chocolate shops, Chocolat Chocolat is a 'must visit' stop on any trip to Cambridge, it's a place where you can watch a deluge of delicious delights being created in front of your eyes as well as sampling the recipe of the day.

Chocolat Chocolat: the home of handmade chocolate...

Chocolat Chocolat

Chocolat Chocolat
SALTED CARAMEL TRUFFLES

Makes 30–40 chocolates.

Ingredients

175ml whipping cream

400g Chocolat Chocolat chocolate buttons

5g sea salt (1 level teaspoon)

Good quality cocoa powder, for dusting

Method

Place the buttons in a glass bowl over a pan of gently simmering water until melted, and then take off the pan.

In a small saucepan, mix the cream and the sea salt and then bring to the boil. Simmer for 1 minute and then leave to cool slightly for about 3 minutes.

Pour the cream onto the melted chocolate, stirring it in gently but quickly, until the ganache is smooth and glossy.

Let the ganache cool for 15-20 minutes and then cover and leave in the fridge for at least 3 hours to set, or overnight if possible.

When the ganache is set, spoon out truffle sized amounts of the mixture and place onto a baking sheet or tray covered with a sheet of greaseproof paper.

Place back in the fridge for 15 minutes.

Drop a truffle into a small bowl of cocoa powder and roll it around gently with a spoon until completely coated.

Place the dusted truffles onto a clean sheet of greaseproof paper.

Eat and enjoy within 3-4 days.

Chocolatier's Notes:

Always melt chocolate using a Bain-Marie or double saucepan.

Never let the water boil or touch the base of your glass bowl as this will burn your chocolate.

Do not allow steam to discolour the chocolate.

Do not add water or fat to chocolate unless the recipe specifies this.

Do not pour boiling cream onto chocolate.

Roll the truffles quickly in your hands or they will begin to melt and lose their shape.

Store the finished truffles in an airtight container in a cool place.

It's a KIND OF MAGIC

Offering a dining setting akin to Hogwarts, Clare College is simply enchanting...

Residing in stunning grounds, spanning both sides of the River Cam, Clare College was founded in 1326 and is the second oldest college in the university.

A truly delightful dining destination, the College offers multiple beautiful rooms for everything from weddings and barbecues, to intimate dinner parties and banquets from two people to 1200. No job is too big or too small.

The multi award-winning team of wizards in the kitchen utilise progressive modern cooking techniques to produce eye catching dishes jam-packed with flavour with the vast amount of ingredients locally sourced.

Seasonality is key, with the experienced multi award-winning team (they've nabbed the Stewards' Cup in the Cambridge Culinary Competition numerous times) only using the freshest products they can get their talented hands on.

Here, they're not only passionate about food, but also the environment, operating a low energy footprint and strongly advocating a fully traceable 'from source to plate' approach to proceedings.

Working closely with clients, dishes such as seared scallops with Jerusalem artichoke purée and crisps, raw and pickled Granny Smith apple, shaved chestnut to start, through to guinea fowl, sage and Parma ham ballotine with leg meat tortellini, squash purée, sprouting broccoli, pavé potato, sage and poultry jus await – all expertly prepared and executed. What's more, opulent guest rooms are available should you decide to extend your visit.

Picturesque, grandiose and downright magical, Clare College will undoubtedly cast a spell on you...

Clare College
VANILLA CONFIT SALMON

with crispy skin, lime emulsion and pickled vegetables.

Ingredients

Components:

Confit salmon

Lime emulsion

Pickled carrot, beetroot, shemji mushroom (any seasonal vegetables)

Slow cooked button onion

Baked beetroot

Sliced radish

Sautéed samphire

Picked chervil

120g piece of salmon

For the vanilla oil:

1 vanilla pod

100ml rapeseed oil (scrape pod and mix with oil)

For the fish cure mix:

50g sugar, 50g salt, star anise, zest of orange, vanilla pod shell, all blended to a powder

For the pickle:

Carrot, beetroot, shimeji mushroom

50ml white wine vinegar

25g sugar

Aromatics of your choice

For the lime emulsion:

2 pasteurised egg yolks

100ml rapeseed oil

1 lime, zest and juice

1 gram Dijon mustard

For the baked beetroot:

Oil

Thyme

Baby beetroot

Method

Coat the salmon in cure mix and leave for 20 minutes. Wash and pat dry, then place into a vacuum pack bag with the vanilla oil. Cook at 45°c for 26 minutes, then place in a bowl with ice cubes to cool. Store until needed.

Combine the vinegar, sugar and aromatics and bring to the boil, strain liquor directly onto the vegetables and cover. Leave until cold.

For the lime emulsion, whisk the egg yolks with the mustard and slowly add the rapeseed oil. Whisk until emulsified, season and finish with the juice and zest of one lime.

Wrap the beetroot, oil and thyme in foil lined with parchment paper, cook in an oven at 175°c until tender. While hot, peel the skin and keep until needed.

To plate, place the salmon in the centre of the plate, pipe three dots of emulsion and build pickled vegetables around, finish with chervil.

Park LIFE

The historic Croxton Park Estate is home to some of the happiest animals
on the planet...

Running organically since 1999, the sprawling Croxton Park Estate is a traditional mixed farm focusing primarily on cows and sheep… with a few pigs who spend their summers in the woods thrown in for good measure.

Native breeds are the buzzword here. Their beef herd is Shorthorn (which is known for doing well off grass and having a superior flavour) whilst two types of specialist sheep also roam the land.

Lleyn sheep from Wales are a more commercial breed of sheep known for being good mothers. Herdwicks from Cumbria are traditional hill sheep which make use of the poorer areas of grassland, take longer to finish, and so have a stronger flavour.

The Oxford Sandy and Black pigs, meanwhile, are good mothers and not overfat like some other rare breeds – and taste absolutely amazing

Hosting regular school visits, the passionate staff engage people directly, informing them about the field to plate process and are involved in environmental stewardship schemes to encourage maximum biodiversity.

The aim at Croxton Park Estate is to farm in a way that respects the land, the animals and the people that work there. In turn, by giving their animals the best possible life, the animals give them delicious, tasty, healthy meat – which they're then generous enough to share with the lucky Cambridgeshire public.

Croxton Park are regular award-winners, for meat made the right way...

Croxton Park
RAGU

This recipe feeds the five thousand with a little Italian flair. Plus, the sauce lasts for five days in the refrigerator or can be frozen.

A tip is to make it the day before consumption. It tastes so much better.

The ingredients make enough pasta sauce for 8-10 people but if you want to make less just cut the ingredient quantities in half.

Our favourite pasta for this dish is penne – but it works equally well with spaghetti.

Ingredients

1kg Croxton Park organically reared minced beef

4 Croxton Park organically reared pork sausages

680g jar Italian tomato passata sauce

2 x 400g cans Italian chopped tomatoes

2 medium white onions, finely chopped

2 medium carrots, finely chopped

2 sticks celery, finely chopped

2 cloves garlic, finely chopped

2 tsp freshly chopped thyme

2 tsp freshly ground nutmeg

250ml white wine or vermouth

2 glasses milk

Salt and pepper for seasoning

Big glug of olive oil

Pasta

Parmesan cheese

Method

In a large pan, preferably a cast iron one, pour in a generous amount of olive oil and fry the finely chopped onions for about 5 minutes. Then add the finely chopped carrots and celery and fry gently for another 5 minutes.

While this is happening, de-skin the sausages and chop in to four or five pieces.

Add to the vegetables and fry until the sausage meat is lightly browned. The meat will crumble into small pieces

Add the finely chopped garlic and thyme then cook for a further minute.

Now add the minced beef and cook and stir until all the meat is browned.

Add the wine or vermouth and cook vigorously for a few minutes to dissipate the alcohol.

Turn down the heat, add the milk and nutmeg, stir and simmer for a few minutes to gently poach the meat and reduce the sauce volume.

Add the passata and cans of tomatoes, salt and pepper to taste, stir and simmer very gently for 1½-2 hours over a low heat with the lid of the pan off at all times. If the sauce looks too thick, add a little water and stir every 20 minutes.

Boil your pasta according to instructions on the packet and serve in a big pasta bowl with many spoonfuls of the ragu and lashings of freshly grated Parmesan cheese.

Accompany with a nice green salad. Here we used mixed leaves, baby broad beans, asparagus and fresh herbs. Tends to go down well with the adults but ignored by the children!

Buon Appetito!

Respect your ELDERS...

From bountiful breakfasts to bundles of beer, Elder Street Café and Deli
is your one-stop-shop to happiness...

Following a successful career in some of the UK's most prestigious hotels and restaurants, Anna and former 2AA rosette chef Gregg Thorne established Elder Street Café and Deli in June 2012.

The business demonstrates the pair's passion for food and drink, behind each product or café dish there's a story linked to their experiences and travels.

Their ethos is to produce as much as possible on site and, what they don't produce they source within the region – endeavouring to offer customers speciality fine food at an affordable price.

Located in Debden, just outside the picturesque market town of Saffron Walden on the Cambridge border, it's a family orientated venue.

Gregg's menu is designed to be fun, educational and encourage customers to share. Seasonal, and flexible where possible, it offers twists on classic dishes, with everything cooked to order from fresh ingredients – plus, the kitchen cures its own fish.

The deli stocks a plethora of local products such as cold pressed rapeseed oil and organic buffalo meat from Thunderley Hall Farm, along with 25 regional cheeses and they even produce their own homemade lemonade. A farmers' market is on the first Saturday of every month and a 'Pork and Cyder Festival' takes place every August Bank Holiday.

A further unique aspect of the deli is their 'Beer Library', stocking over 200 bottled real ales from breweries and micro-breweries located in the region.

Friendly, fun and a firm favourite with locals be sure to pop along and respect your Elders...

Elder Street Café & Deli
ORGANIC BUFFALO BURGERS

The organic buffalo is sourced from Thunderley Hall Farm – which is located less than half a mile from the business. The chorizo is sourced from Lane Farm, Brundish, and the smoked garlic from the Isle of Wight Garlic Farm – Gregg's place of birth. Makes 6 burgers.

Ingredients

For the burgers:

1kg organic buffalo mince

200g Suffolk chorizo, finely diced

2 dsp tomato ketchup

1 dsp Worcestershire sauce

1 free range egg yolk

1 tsp cracked black pepper

1 bunch flat leaf parsley, chopped

1 small red onion, finely diced

For the mayonnaise:

4 tbsp mayonnaise

½ tsp English mustard

Juice ½ lemon

2 cloves Isle of Wight smoked garlic, peeled

For the garnish:

6 brioche burger buns

3 vine plum tomatoes, sliced

1 red onion, sliced into rings

2 buffalo mozzarella sliced

Wild rocket leaves

To serve:

Homemade coleslaw

Beer battered onion rings

Method

For the mayonnaise

Place all of the ingredients into a food processor, blend until fully combined.

For the burgers

In a large mixing bowl combine all the ingredients, mixing thoroughly.

Firmly press the mix into a 10cm x 2cm metal ring to form a patty.

Cover with cling film and refrigerate overnight.

Preheat the oven to 200°c, heat a char grill, griddle or frying pan until it just begins to smoke.

With a little vegetable oil, oil the burger on both sides – not the pan. Seal the burgers for approximately 2 minutes on each side.

Remove from the pan and place in the oven for a further 5 minutes to achieve a slightly pink centre. Halfway through the cooking time, melt a couple of slices of buffalo mozzarella on top of each burger.

Don't discard the griddle. Cut each brioche burger bun in half and lightly toast in the burger juices.

To serve

Layer the base of the burger bun with sliced vine plum tomato, red onion rings and wild rocket leaves, top with the burgers and a healthy dollop of the smoked garlic and lemon mayonnaise.

Accompany with homemade coleslaw and beer battered onion rings.

Stop, PRESS!

Read all about it...

A traditional backstreet public house within walking distance of the heart of historic Cambridge, The Free Press has been a pub for over 120 years, and is now run by Craig and Jenna Bickley.

Before then, a part of the premises was used as a printing press for a free Cambridge newspaper, and despite only lasting one issue, the name stuck.

A true test of character, the pub has managed to withstand some turbulent times – in the 1970s it was closed and marked for demolition as the whole area was to be redeveloped. However, a successful campaign managed to save it, and the pub has remained largely unchanged ever since.

A warm and cosy establishment with an open fire, snug and courtyard garden, The Free Press is decorated with pages of old newspapers and printing trays, which customers can fill with keep sakes. The pub serves an ever-changing selection of real ales, and has a large collection of gin, malt whisky and bottled beer.

But it's not all about the tasty tipples on offer; The Free Press Kitchen is run by siblings Megan and Thomas Stepney. All of the food on offer is homemade and freshly prepared using predominately locally sourced produce.

Although a seasonal and evolving menu, The Free Press continue to serve ever-popular staples including their famous Scotch eggs, doorstep sandwiches, hand-pressed burgers and beer-battered fish and chips. Portions are generous, and to complement the food, the pub's spectacular service means they are only too happy to cater for individual needs.

Together Jenna, Craig and Megan add to the wonderful homely and welcoming atmosphere of the pub.

The Free Press
BLACK PUDDING SCOTCH EGG

With smoky tomato chutney.

Ingredients

For the Scotch egg:

120g good quality sausage meat
(head to your local butcher)

40g diced black pudding

10g coriander

A pinch of salt and pepper

¼ red chilli, deseeded

1 fresh free-range egg

Flour, for dusting

1 egg, for coating

Homemade breadcrumbs – we use
day old bread, blended in a food
processor and toasted in the oven
until golden brown.

For the Smoky tomato chutney:

Splash of olive oil

2 red onions, chopped finely

3 garlic cloves, crushed

4 tbsp smoked paprika

2 red chillies, chopped

½ pint red wine vinegar

600g brown sugar

2kg tomatoes, chopped

1 tbsp ground cumin

Salt

Method

For the Scotch egg

Using an egg at room temperature, boil for 5 minutes 45 seconds to ensure a runny yolk.

Put the egg into iced cold water.

Once cooled peel and then flour – this helps the meat stick to the egg.

Mix the sausage meat, diced black pudding, salt and pepper, finely sliced coriander and chopped chilli.

Wrap the egg in your sausage meat mixture carefully so as not to break it.

Lay out three bowls, one of flour, one of beaten egg, and one of breadcrumbs.

Coat the egg and sausage meat in flour, dusting off any excess, then dip in the beaten egg, then finally in the breadcrumbs.

We fry our eggs at 180°c for 10 minutes, but they can also be baked.

For the Smokey tomato chutney

Heat olive oil in a large pan on a medium heat, sauté onions and garlic until soft.

Add smoked paprika, cumin, chillies, brown sugar and a pinch of salt and stir until the sugar has dissolved leaving a chutney like texture.

Add the chopped tomatoes and red wine vinegar, bring to the boil for 20 minutes and then lower the heat to simmer and cook for 2 hours. Stirring occasionally.

Leave to cool and store in sterilised glass jars until ready to serve.

This recipe makes 1.5 litres.

By GEORGE!

Old meets new at The George Hotel and Brasserie – resulting in the ultimate boutique experience.

Owned by the Furbank family since 2003, The George Hotel and Brasserie is a stunning former coaching inn which has lovingly been brought up to date whilst staying true to its heritage.

The highest rated three star boutique hotel in the heart of Cambridgeshire, this bustling wine bar and 2AA rosette brasserie are popular hangouts for drinkers and diners angling for top notch service.

The George Hotel offers casual dining throughout the day and night, seven days a week. During the summer months, al fresco dining is also available on the beautiful terrace. From cooked and continental breakfasts, to à la carte offerings such as roast Browning Farm duck breast with celeriac purée, dauphinoise potatoes, savoy cabbage, confit grapes and lemon thyme jus, or pan-fried fillet of plaice with Austell Bay mussels, sautéed new potatoes, buttered spinach and tomato salsa, The George delivers quality across the board. What's more, delicious cream teas are served everyday between 3pm and 5pm and the Sunday lunches are super popular.

For wine lovers, there's an incredible selection available. 20 house wines are on offer by the glass – whilst there's another 100 plus wines from all over the world to suit every palate.

Aside from the food and drink, The George also offers twelve beautifully designed bedrooms all characterised after their namesake of a famous 'George'.

If you're after a high calibre, boutique experience, this multi award-winner will tick every box…

George Hotel & Brasserie

the GEORGE
HOTEL & BRASSERIE

Harrison

The George

ROASTED FILLET OF WILD SEA BASS

With Israeli couscous, brown shrimps, clams, peas, broad beans and lemon
butter sauce. Serves 2.

Ingredients

2 sea bass fillets

1 garlic clove

50g broad beans

50g fresh peas

50g clams

50g brown shrimps, cooked

30g Israeli couscous

1 bottle white wine

60g unsalted butter

60g double cream

40g lemon juice

Pea shoots, baby watercress and
chives, to garnish

Salt and pepper

Olive oil

Method

For the Israeli couscous, fill a small saucepan two thirds with water; add salt and a little olive oil, then bring to the boil. Add the couscous and simmer for 8 minutes until the couscous is al dente.

Prepare and blanch the broad beans and peas and refresh in ice water.

Prepare the sea bass and season on both sides with salt and pepper. Heat a small amount of oil in a frying pan, add the fish and fry over a medium heat for about 3 minutes. Add 10g of butter and place in the oven at 180°c for another 4 minutes. Keep warm.

For the lemon butter sauce place 250ml white wine in a saucepan on a medium heat and simmer for 5 minutes. Add the double cream and butter, and simmer until thickened. Add the cooked shrimp then add the lemon juice.

To cook the clams, heat a pan and add a tablespoon of oil, the clams, a glug of white wine and garlic and cover until the shells start to open.

To serve, place the couscous onto a dish followed by the sea bass, then the clams, broad beans and peas. Add chopped chives to the sauce, pour over and garnish with pea shoots and baby watercress.

Oh, Magog
I CAN'T BELIEVE IT

You can't be all things to everyone, but at Gog Magog Hills,
they come pretty darn close...

Farm shop, butchery, kitchen, café, deli – brothers Charles and Marcus Bradford have created Gog Magog Hills to be your one-stop shop for stunning Cambridgeshire produce across the board.

Based on Heath Farm, a couple of miles south of Cambridge, quality, taste and provenance is top of the list here, and they have a ton of fun while they're at it.

The deli and farm shop are home to a host of foodie treasures, be it fresh fruit and veg, brilliant British cheeses, or even a range of homemade ready meals all made with only the finest ingredients, of course.

At the award-winning butchery, home of 'England's Best Burger', they take immense pride in their meat – always ensuring excellent animal husbandry and welfare. It's an integral part of the farm and they really know their stuff. Any questions, the friendly team will always be on hand to help you make the most of their meat.

The social hub at 'The Gogs' is the café – where you're guaranteed a warm welcome, great coffee and cracking cakes. It's the perfect place to sit and recharge your batteries or enjoy a chat over the numerous cookery books.

Then there's The Shack. Bringing the great outdoors indoors, it's a fab space to enjoy their wonderful cuisine in a different setting. Especially suited to dog walkers and cyclists, be it sunny or cold, The Shack delivers big time – especially at weekends which often sees their barbecue and some of Cambridge's best street food being served.

The kitchen concludes the line-up, where fresh food is made from scratch every day. From award-winning cheese scones, and Scotch eggs through to winter-warming soups, sandwiches and fresh summer salads, the team consistently raise the bar with new recipes and the best seasonal produce...

Gog Magog Hills

Gog Magog Hills
COOLEA & GARLIC MUSHROOM TART

This deceptively simple tartlet is hugely popular at Gog Magog Hills. The key is to use the best quality cheeses you can, something with a real punch that loves to be melted like a mature Gouda, or Coolea Farmhouse cheese.

Stay away from cheddar as it will make the pastry oily.

Serve with a fresh crunchy chopped salad or slaw to balance out the pastry.

Makes 1 tartlet, but this can be multiplied up to make a family sized tart.

Ingredients

65g puff pastry (feel free to use ready-made)

45g Coolea (or Gouda) cheese, thinly sliced

40g button mushrooms, thinly sliced

Egg wash

Knob of butter

Method

Cut the pastry into a 12cm square.

Leaving a 2cm border, cut a smaller square inside.

Now for the tricky bit – pick up two opposite corners, bring them together in the middle and thread one corner under the other. The border should now be the same size as the square.

Stick the border to the base using egg wash.

Prick the middle with a fork to stop it puffing up.

Cook in the oven for 10 minutes at 180°c.

While the pastry case cools, soften the mushrooms in the butter over a medium heat.

At this point you can have a play, feel free to add to the pan any other flavours you fancy, like dried herbs, ham, bacon, coarsely ground pepper, chopped garlic… it's up to you.

Place half of the Coolea in the tart.

Add all of the mushrooms and top with the remaining cheese.

Bake again at 180°c for 6 minutes until the cheese has melted and looks amazing.

a SHOE-INN

A beloved village institution, the award-winning Horseshoe Inn continues to stand the test of time...

The Horseshoe Inn has stood in the picturesque Cambridgeshire village of Offord D'Arcy (between St Neots and Godmanchester) since 1626. Initially a Yeoman's cottage, it's seen many changes and had many functions over the years – latterly the village Inn.

In its current incarnation, 'The Shoe' as it's affectionately known by its patrons, is a spacious gastropub with two inglenook fireplaces and an extensive family-friendly garden.

Owned and operated by the Kennedy family for many years, this welcoming establishment successfully combines an old village pub with a gourmet restaurant. The 390-year old period building has been extended but retains much of the original features and charm, with the bars boasting low ceilings in a rustic style with exposed beams along with several real ales and ciders.

Voted the area's 'most loved' business for five years running, and with several awards over the last few years, but what The Shoe is really renowned for is its food.

Combining traditional homemade pub classics, with more adventurous dishes chef patron Richard and his long standing kitchen team of Andrew, Mary, Brett and Ross, utilise locally sourced seasonal ingredients to produce honest rustic English countryside style food with an imaginative twist – influenced by their wealth of experience – from Michelin-starred and multi rosette restaurants to 50 years of home cooking. This is what makes their food special.

With dishes such as porcini mushroom with fontina arancini and toasted oat rolled haggis Scotch eggs to start, to loin of local rabbit in Pancetta with ale braised rabbit leg sausage roll and smoky maple glazed duck leg with sweet potato, chilli and baby kale hash for the main course, you can see why this place features so heavily on many folks' food radar...

Horseshoe Inn
GRILLED TUNA

With chilli, garlic, oregano in borlotti beans with roasted red pepper stew
and courgette ribbons. Serves 4.

Ingredients

For the tuna:

4 x 200g tuna loin steaks

1 tsp dried chilli flakes

1 lemon, juiced

2 garlic cloves, crushed

4 tbsp extra virgin olive oil

2 tbsp water

2 tbsp chopped oregano

For the stew:

2 red peppers

2 onions, finely diced

2 carrots, finely diced

1 stick celery, finely diced

2 garlic cloves, crushed

2 tbsp olive oil

800g (2 tins) borlotti beans, drained
and rinsed

800g (2 tins) chopped tomatoes

1 bunch basil, leaves torn

For the courgette ribbons:

2 courgettes

1 tbsp extra virgin olive oil

1 lemon, zested

Seasoning

Method

Preheat the oven to 200°c.

In a bowl whisk the water and olive oil until thick and creamy. Whisk in the lemon juice with a few pinches of salt, then add the chilli flakes, crushed garlic, and chopped oregano. Brush over the tuna steaks and leave to marinate while preparing the stew.

Brush red peppers with olive oil and roast in oven for 15-20 minutes until the skins have blackened and blistered. Remove from the oven, place in a bowl and cover with cling film (whilst still hot). Once cooled, take the peppers and remove the blistered skin, then cut the flesh into long thin strips.

To make the stew

Heat olive oil over a medium heat until hot and add the onions, carrot and celery and sweat off for 2-3 minutes until softened, add the crushed garlic and cook for another 2 minutes. Add the chopped tomatoes and borlotti beans and bring to the boil. Simmer for 20 minutes, then add the roasted pepper strips, torn basil leaves and check the seasoning. Keep warm.

Place a saucepan of water on to boil with a good pinch of salt.

For the courgette ribbons

Take the top and bottom off the courgettes and using a peeler, peel strips of courgette going from top to bottom. Place the ribbons into boiling water for 30 seconds and drain in a colander, toss with olive oil, lemon zest and season to taste.

To cook the tuna

Heat a griddle pan until smoking hot and sear the tuna on each side for 1-2 minutes (depending on thickness of the fish).

To assemble

Place a bed of the bean stew in the centre of each plate and top with the tuna steak and the courgette ribbons. Finish with a drizzle of olive oil.

Hot in
THE KITCHEN

Delivering restaurant quality cuisine, directly to your own front door, Inder's Kitchen could very well be your new best friend...

The seed for Inder's Kitchen was planted when Inder herself was on maternity leave in London. Unable to get to a quality restaurant, she ordered a takeaway and was incredibly disappointed at what turned up.

Why should she have to compromise on quality just because she had to stay at home? Hence, Inder's Kitchen was born.

Dishing up only the finest Indian cuisine to Cambridge residents since 2010, everything on the menu is cooked to order using fresh, locally sourced produce with spices which they grind and blend themselves.

It's restaurant quality cooking which you can enjoy from the comfort of your own home. Adopting a seasonal ethos along with regular specials focussing on different regions of India and showcasing the diversity of the country.

Aiming to deliver within 30 minute timeslots (free, of course), customers can enjoy the likes of Amritsari fish pakoras or pepper and chilli crusted chicken to start, followed by main courses like chicken Xacuti and Peshwari mutton curry. A range of handmade chutneys are available to complement the cuisine – as well as a host of top notch frozen ready meals for further convenience.

Inder's Kitchen also offers event and party catering, from cosy dinner parties to weddings, corporate events and more as well as frequent diner rewards – simply register when you order to benefit from a 10% discount on future orders.

For a true taste of India, delivered directly and swiftly to your own front door, give Inder and her team a tinkle or order online at inderskitchen.com.

Inder's Kitchen
KERALAN CHICKEN CURRY

Ingredients

1kg boneless diced chicken thigh

50ml vegetable oil

½ stick cinnamon

1 tsp cloves

1 tsp green cardamom pods

2 dried bay leaves

1 tsp fennel seeds

1 tsp mustard seeds

4 dried red Kashmiri chillies

6 sliced Spanish white onions

1 tbsp ginger & garlic paste

1½ tsp red chilli powder

2 tsp coriander powder

1½ tsp turmeric powder

400g tin chopped tomatoes

1 can coconut milk

1 tbsp garam masala

Salt for seasoning

Method

Heat the oil in a pan.

Fry the dry spices until they crackle and pop.

Add the sliced onions and sweat, stirring occasionally, until they start to brown.

Place in the ginger and garlic paste. Stir well and frequently to prevent sticking until the mixture is a dark, golden brown colour.

Then add the powdered spices, stir well and allow to cook for a further minute.

Empy in the tinned tomatoes and cook for 5 minutes.

Add the chicken and coconut milk and cook until the chicken is just cooked.

Sprinkle on the garam masala and salt to taste.

I scream, you scream
WE ALL SCREAM FOR...

A culinary wizard, Jack van Praag has been conjuring up magical concoctions at Jack's Gelato since 2010.

Jack van Praag is the man behind Jack's Gelato – *the* place to head for expertly crafted ice creams and sorbets.

Born and raised in Cambridge, Jack's career in food was a gap year that luckily never ended. He's plied his trade in top kitchens across the world, over the years working his way up from apprentice to an award-winning head chef.

Now he's back in Cambridge, sharing the love with his hometown in the form of Jack's Gelato.

On an average day you'll find him behind his counter at Nord on Sussex Street or manning his ice-tricycle, scoop in hand, ready to make your day (find out where on Twitter @jacks_gelato). On the average night you'll find him in the kitchen, churning up new batches of the cold stuff.

Chalked on the blackboard and changing daily, there's a lineup of flavours from the vanilla you'll feel you've waited your whole life for, to more inventive flavours like goats' milk and wild honey or the refreshing cucumber, apple and gin sorbet.

It's this care and inventiveness that's won Jack countless devotees – and seen his product stocked in a host of well-loved Cambridgeshire establishments.

Creating everything by hand, Jack uses only the finest quality ingredients which often includes produce from his own allotment.

So, if you're wondering what true genius tastes like, get the full scoop at Jack's Gelato…

Jack's Gelato
RHUBARB SORBET

Makes about 800ml.

This wonderful sorbet works well with forced winter rhubarb as well as outdoor rhubarb. The former is available from Yorkshire, in a number of varieties, and is an amazing winter 'fruit'. The latter is grown all over the UK and in countless gardens and allotments and, to me at least, is one of the key tastes of British summertime.

I often omit the spice and go for a classic full-on rhubarb flavour. I've also successfully made this with various other herbs and spices including cardamom, ginger, orange zest, bay and juniper. You could also substitute the water, or part of it, with some leftover Prosecco or the like (does Champagne ever get left over?)

If you don't have an ice cream machine, or even if you do, you may prefer to make a granita. Simply still freeze it and as it firms up scrape it with a fork to form a classic granita consistency. Serve with some crème chantilly or even simply some plain whipped cream.

Ingredients

300g rhubarb stalks

350ml water

250g sugar

40 Szechuan peppercorns

Pinch of Maldon sea salt

Splash of vodka (optional)

Method

Heat the water, sugar and peppercorns and allow to gently simmer for 3-5 minutes. Remove, cover and set aside. Leave to infuse for at least 15 minutes. Strain.

Wash the rhubarb and remove the leaves. Chop the stalks into pieces and add to the spice infusion, along with the sugar. Bring to a simmer and cook until the rhubarb has completely softened. Do not let it boil vigorously.

Cover and set aside and allow to cool. Blend with a hand blender or jug blender.

Season with a pinch of salt and a splash of vodka, if using.

Churn in an ice cream machine or freeze as it is and remove periodically to stir and beat all the ice crystals out of it until it forms the desired consistency.

Serve as soon as possible!

To the
MANOR BORN

There's a whole lot of goodness waiting behind the door of
The Larder at Burwash Manor...

From tiny acorns, great oaks grow. It's hard to believe that The Larder we know and love today, originally began life as a small concrete shed on the Radford's farm – Burwash Manor's own asparagus and sweetcorn was on display along with a simple honesty box.

Now, a renowned foodie destination with over 3,000 products adorning their burgeoning shelves, The Larder is beginning to realise farmer Michael Radford's dream of owning the best delicatessen in East Anglia.

The working organic farm (which holds the highest level of stewardship for conservation) is also home to a group of converted farm buildings just off the M11 in Cambridge. These buildings house a selection of 15 wonderful independent businesses, including a florist, a haberdashery, day spa and a new eatery run by Romano's from December 2015.

The secret to Burwash Larder's success is a simple one – passion. The basic philosophy here is to sell the very best produce from the county and beyond.

From organic fruit and vegetables through to a buckling cheese counter, a master butcher, smoked fish and meats, cakes, bread, biscuits and beyond, The Larder truly lives up to its name. You'll leave with bags full of fare and a massive smile on your face. Don't forget to pick up their ever-popular rare breed sausages and bacon made from pigs on the farm.

A thoroughly immersive and relaxing experience, you can even choose a filled roll or famous sausage roll to enjoy with a locally-roasted coffee on the sun terrace after you've exhausted the kids on one of the nature walks.

The friendly and attentive staff are always on hand to offer advice or point you in the direction of their favourite products; you'll also find local suppliers sampling their produce at the weekends as well as guest food vans and chef friend Ursula Ferrigno serving up delicious food out on the terrace.

For fun on the farm, fill your boots at The Larder...

Burwash Manor
PORK TENDERLOIN

And asparagus baked in pastry (Filetto di maiale e prosciutto in crosta.) Serves 6.
This is a stylish presentation for pork and asparagus. It can be prepared in advance
and kept in the wings ready to go.

Ingredients

450g pork tenderloin fillet

Sea salt and freshly ground black pepper

3 tsp rosemary, finely chopped

100g fine fresh asparagus

8 slices Parma ham

1 large egg, beaten for the glaze

For the pastry:

200g '00' grade flour

Pinch of salt

100g unsalted butter, diced

2 tbsp ice cold water, to bind

Method

Preheat the oven to 190°c.

Firstly, make the pastry. Mix the flour and salt together, then rub in the butter until it resembles breadcrumbs. Add enough water to bind into a damp ball. Wrap in cling film and refrigerate for 20 minutes.

Lightly season the meat and sprinkle with rosemary. Then wrap the asparagus and ham around the meat – the ham should overlap – then place on a baking sheet.

Roll the pastry out to the length of the pork and drape the pastry over the pork, tucking it in under the meat. It doesn't need to be completely sealed.

Brush with the beaten egg and chopped rosemary if desired, and bake for 40 minutes, until the pastry is golden.

Allow the meat to relax for about 15 minutes before slicing. Serve without a sauce.

Eat, Drink and BE MERRY

Familiar fodder given a cheeky twist is the order of the day at The Merry Monk...

Hidden snuggly away amongst the Cambridgeshire Fens, The Merry Monk originally began life as three cottages in the 17th Century before becoming The Red Lion public house until 1992 whereupon it adopted its current moniker.

Husband and wife team Adrian and Michelle Smith have been the tour de force behind the popular Isleham watering hole since 2002 – lovingly restoring the once rundown public house yet retaining pretty period features such as sash windows and oak beams.

Atmosphere here is the key, with a roaring log fire on colder days along with a thoroughly charming beer garden during sunnier climes.

With an interesting mix of locals and visitors, it's an informal, yet effortlessly stylish drinking and dining destination.

A fabulous range of wines, beers and spirits awaits – but it's the food here that really gets people talking. Accommodating up to sixty people across three separate rooms for lunch and dinner.

The seasonal menu utilises fresh, local produce. Be it a bowl of mussels from the marshes at Brancaster, or delicious asparagus picked in fields a few minutes away. Everything from haggis in beer batter with whisky and mustard mayonnaise to nibble, through to pan fried calves liver with bacon, buttered spring onion mash, confit roasted onion and Madeira for your main is available. It's inspired cooking of the highest order. Oh, and let's not forget the stunning Sunday lunches.

The Merry Monk is a place where everyone gets the VIP treatment...

BEERS, CIDERS + PORTERS

APPISTES ROCHEFORT (9.2%) £4.60 330ml
ST MALLE TRAPPIST TRIPLE (9.5%) £4.80 330ml
NAMS SOUTHWOLD DRY HOP LAGER (4.2%) £3.80
RELLA DAMM HIGH (4.6%) £3.60
EAM STOUT (6.5%) £4.20 500ml
PETER'S HONEY PORTER (4.5%) £3.70 500ml
TEFANUS BLONDE (7%) £5.50 330ml
PERS PALE ALE (4.5%) £4.50 375ml
HARD PIG CIDER (4.5%) £5.00 500ml
NEY'S DRY CIDER (6%) £4.20 500ml

...NEW!...

GUINNESS DUBLIN PORTER
(3.8%) 500ml £4.50

GUINNESS WEST INDIES
PORTER
(6.0%) 500ml £5.00

The Merry Monk
JACOBS LADDER BEEF SHORT RIBS

Beer and treacle slow-roasted beef short ribs, horseradish mash and braised buttered carrots.

Ingredients

Olive oil

3 medium onions, peeled and chopped

2 cloves garlic, peeled and chopped

2 carrots, peeled and chopped

2 sticks celery, sliced

4 portobello mushrooms, peeled

3kg meaty beef short ribs (Jacobs ladder)

A few sprigs fresh thyme, chopped

A few fresh bay leaves

Pinch of salt

1 tsp freshly cracked black pepper for seasoning

500ml beer

2 tbsp treacle

Butter

For the mash potato with horseradish and parsley:

1kg potatoes (Agra are best if possible), peeled and cut lengthwise into quarters

½ teaspoon salt

60ml heavy cream

30g butter

1 tbsp milk (or more)

Salt and pepper

50g freshly grated horseradish

50ml white wine vinegar

25g sugar

Bunch of parsley, chopped

For the buttered braised carrots:

10 medium carrots peeled, topped and tailed

250g butter

150g sugar

3 tsp salt

Bunch of fresh thyme

Method

Preheat the oven to 150°c.

Heat a tablespoon of olive oil in a large ovenproof pan on a low heat.

Add the chopped onions and fry gently for about 10 minutes until nice and soft (don't let them colour too much).

Turn the heat up, then add the garlic, butter, carrots, celery and mushrooms. Mix everything together before adding the chopped thyme, bay leaves and salt then place the ribs on top

Brown for a few minutes, then pour in the beer. Stir, and add just enough water to cover. Bring to a simmer, add the black pepper and cover with a lid or tin foil. Cook in the oven for about 4½ hours, giving it a look from time to time. The ribs should have tender meat in a rich, dark, thick stew.

Place the pan on the stove top then add the treacle, reduce until it thickens further, then baste the ribs and cook for 40-45 minutes – basting every 5 minutes or so.

Rest for 20 minutes in a warm place.

Serve with cooking juice and vegetables left in the pan.

For the mash potato with horseradish and parsley

Finely grate the horseradish and soak in the vinegar and sugar for 20 minutes, then drain and squeeze out the liquid. Set aside for later.

Place the peeled and cut potatoes into a medium saucepan. Add cold water to the pan until the potatoes are covered. Add a half teaspoon of salt to the water. Turn the heat on to high and bring the water to a boil.

Reduce the heat to low to maintain a simmer and cover. Cook for 15-20 minutes, or until you can easily poke through them with a fork.

While the potatoes are cooking, melt the butter and warm the cream. You can heat them together in a pan.

When the potatoes are done, drain the water well so they're as dry as possible, place the steaming potatoes into a large bowl and pour the heated cream and melted butter over the potatoes. Mash the potatoes with a potato masher, then use a strong wooden spoon to beat further. Add milk and beat until the mashed potatoes are smooth. Add salt and pepper to taste and the grated horseradish. Finish with chopped parsley.

For the buttered braised carrots

Use a clean scourer or peeler to peel the carrots.

In a pan, combine 400ml of water, the butter, sugar, salt and thyme. Bring to the boil, then reduce the heat to a gentle simmer and add the carrots. Cook for around 35 minutes until the carrots are tender and the liquid has reduced by about half.

Serve the carrots as a side dish with the reduced cooking liquid poured over.

A Midsummer
NIGHT'S DREAM

With two Michelin stars, and one of the country's finest chefs at the helm in
Daniel Clifford, it's fair to say that Cambridge's Midsummer House
is living the culinary dream...

The year of 1998 saw Midsummer House handing over its reins to renowned chef Daniel Clifford. He had one dream – to turn the beautiful Victorian premises into Cambridgeshire's best restaurant.

Two Michelin stars later (2002 and 2005), with a host of plaudits under his belt, including 5AA rosettes and a couple of champion titles on the Great British Menu, it's fair to say his dream has become a stunning reality.

Showing impressive cooking skills at an early age (he was the only boy in his school to take Home Economics and openly admits it was the single class he had any interest in), a course had been set which was to lead him on the incredible journey to where he is today.

Stints with the likes of Jean Bardet in France, Simon Gueller at Rascasse, Leeds and Marco Pierre White at The Box Tree, Ilkley all helped shape Daniel into a blossoming star on the culinary scene.

His time at Midsummer House has seen his potential fully realised as one of the most respected and successful chefs in the UK.

Based in idyllic settings on the banks of the River Cam, life at Midsummer House hasn't always been easy. Two floods, in 1999 and 2000 respectively, nearly called time on proceedings.

But, what doesn't kill you makes you stronger – and following a combination of graft, determination and sheer stubbornness, the award-winning restaurant now holds court at the top of Cambridgeshire's gastronomic tree.

With strong focus on local seasonality, minimalism, natural flavours and exquisite execution, dining at Midsummer House is so much more than just a meal – it's literally living the dream...

Midsummer House
ENGLISH ASPARAGUS

With burnt onion, potatoes, hollandaise sauce.

Ingredients

For the asparagus:

250g chopped asparagus

30g double cream

30g butter

8 large spears of asparagus

For the potato cannelloni:

Two very large chippy choice potatoes

Vegetable oil, for frying

5g potato starch

For the hollandaise sauce:

3 egg yolks

30g white wine vinegar

250g beurre noisette

Salt

Lemon

For the white wine shallot rings:

1 medium shallot, 4mm sliced

100ml white cooking wine

For the cannelloni mixture: (4 portions)

To make the truffled egg white:

100g egg white

2g salt

2g white truffle oil

To make the chestnut mushrooms:

2 large mushrooms, 4mm dice

40g asparagus, 2mm dice

Burnt onion powder (4 portions)

2 white onions, peeled and halved

Method

For the asparagus purée

Season a large pan of boiling water with salt. Add the chopped asparagus and cook for 2 minutes. Bring the cream to the boil. On a low heat melt the butter. Increase the heat and whisk until it turns nut brown in colour (beurre noisette). Strain the asparagus well in a sieve. Place all three ingredients into a blender. Blend until smooth. Season with salt and pass the purée through a sieve into a bowl that is sitting on ice to cool it down.

For four of the spears of asparagus, measure 14cm in length and cut. On 11cm score very lightly (this is an indicator where to turn). With a small knife remove the wings of the stem until you have a clean looking tip. Where you made the small mark, score the whole way around the asparagus. Trimming off a 1mm incision into the flesh leaves you with a very clean turned spear of asparagus.

On the other four, remove the wings as before but at 8cm in length. With the trim remove the thin wood. Cut 12 small triangles at 45° angle. Blanch in boiling salty water for 30 seconds. Refresh in ice. Cook the 14cm and 8cm spears in boiling salted water for approximately 2 minutes, until tender.

For the potato cannelloni

Put the potatoes through a mandoline on flat blade. Cut rectangles of potato 13cm by 8cm. Once cut, blanch for a couple of seconds in a fryer at 160°c or until it becomes more flexible. Season while it is still hot. Dab with paper to remove the excess oil. Make a paste using the potato starch and a little water. Lay the potato slice on your board. On the top of the potato rub a thin line of paste. Taking a metal tube 1cm in diameter wrap the potato around the tube and push down when it's in contact with the glue making sure it sticks. Place the tubes, once all four are complete, into the oil at 180°c for 1-2 minutes, or until golden brown and very crisp. Remove from the oil. Take the potato off the tube when it's still hot and set aside.

For the hollandaise sauce

Place the egg yolks and vinegar in a round based bowl. Place over a pan of lightly simmering water. Whisk continuously until pale and light. Make sure the eggs do not scramble. Take off the heat and slowly pour in the beurre noisette. Halfway through add a tablespoon of water allowing you to work in all the butter and not split. Season with salt and lemon juice. The sauce should have the consistency of lightly whipped cream – if too thick, let down with water.

Cling film the sauce and place in a warm place until ready to serve.

For the white wine shallot rings

Pick the shallot into individual rings. Cover with white wine and cook gently on low heat until nearly cooked. Allow to cool in the liquid.

For the cannelloni

To make the truffled egg white

Whisk the egg white, salt and white truffle oil together gently. Pour into a greased, lined tray and cook at 90°c for 14 minutes. Chill until set. Dice into 4mm.

To make the chestnut mushrooms

To make the mixture, combine the mushrooms and diced asparagus with the truffled egg white when diced, and mix with asparagus purée (approximately 50g depending on consistency). Season with salt and lemon and put into a piping bag ready to fill the potato cannelloni.

For the burnt onion powder

In a dry pan, place onions on a high heat until blackened all the way through.

Dry in a dehydrator for 24 hours at 130°c.

Blend half at a time in a dry mixer until you get a fine powder.

To assemble the dish

Warm through the asparagus purée. Dress the mushroom discs in olive oil, salt and a thin dusting of onion powder. Warm through the cooked asparagus in seasoned butter. Swipe the purée on the plate. Arrange the asparagus pieces, mushroom slices and shallot rings on one side of the purée. Half fill the cannelloni with the mix. Place the small spear inside. Place on the plate alongside the long spears and serve.

Once upon a time
IN MEXICO

At Nanna Mexico, they believe every great meal should be served with a story.
Are you sitting comfortably? Then we'll begin…

Once upon a time in Mexico there lived a single mother named Margarita – who had seven mouths to feed. It was a tough time, living in cramped conditions, with every day a fight for survival.

But Margarita was a fighter and one day she decided she was not only going to look after her own wonderful family, she was going to look after the whole neighbourhood as well – and from a table in the middle of the Barrio Bravo she worked her magic, turning fresh local market-bought ingredients into fantastic feasts for the local factory workers.

Little did she know at the time that her spirit, passion and devotion would be the inspiration for her grandson Luis' business Nanna Mexico.

At Nanna Mexico, it's more than just delicious authentic food – it's about intense passion, the kind born out of Margarita's hardship on the Mexican streets. Luis wanted to bring his Nanna's Mexico to the UK – the smells, the colours, the tastes, textures and, most importantly, those original ingredients. It's fair to say, he's achieved his vision… and done Nanna proud.

This is the true Mexican experience. Fresh, healthy, nourishing fare such as burritos, enchiladas and quesadillas, made from scratch using quality local produce, with no preservatives.

They've come a long way from a table in the street but the food and ethos remain the same.

Nanna Mexico
CHILES EN NOGADA

This is one of the most traditional dishes in Mexican cuisine – and a personal favorite of mine. My Nanna used to cook this for me on special occasions. So, when I achieved something at school, or I had something to celebrate, my Nanna would take the time to make this beautiful dish to praise me.
The name Nogada comes from the Spanish word for the walnut tree, nogal. The dish consists of poblano peppers filled with sweetened minced beef stuffing and topped with a walnut based cream (Nogada). The final dish features the colors of the Mexican flag; green from the chilli and parsley leaves, white from the walnut cream and red from the pomegranate seeds. Makes 12.

Ingredients

12 chiles poblanos

For the sweet stuffing:

2 tbsp lard

1 onion, chopped

2 garlic cloves, finely chopped

350g minced beef

100g raisins

225g chopped apricots, dates and or figs

4 small cooking apples, peeled, cored and chopped

3 pears, peeled, cored and chopped

500g chopped tomatoes

100g sliced almonds

100g pine nuts

¼ tsp dried thyme

½ tsp Mexican oregano

¾ tsp ground cinnamon

¼ tsp ground clove

For the nogada cream:

800g whole peeled walnuts, soaked in water or frozen to keep from turning brown

170ml thick cream

125ml full fat milk

2 tbsp sherry

2 tbsp sugar

For the garnish:

1 handful chopped parsley leaves

200g pomegranate seeds

Method

Firstly, char the chiles poblanos over a grill or directly on an open flame. Once slightly charred, peel the skin. Open a slice in the chile poblano to stuff it. Leave half an inch at either end so the chile keeps its shape after stuffing. Carefully remove the seeds and set the chiles aside.

If you're using tinned chiles, they won't keep the shape and may tear. Don't worry, try to use them as 'blankets' on top of the stuffing.

For the sweet stuffing

Melt lard in a skillet over medium heat.

Add the onion and cook for 3 minutes.

Add the garlic and stir for a minute.

Add the minced beef and cook stirring occasionally, until the meat changes color and has mostly cooked.

Pour in the chopped tomatoes and bring to a boil. Add raisins, fruit, spices, nuts and a little salt to taste.

Bring to boil, cover and simmer for 30 minutes on low. Fill the chiles without bursting them.

For the nogada cream

Blend the walnuts, cream, milk, sherry and sugar. The sauce should be thick and it should pour slowly.

Serve the chiles poblanos by placing them in the middle of a dish with a ladle of nogada cream covering them. Sprinkle with parsley and pomegranate seeds. Serve at room temperature.

Chef's Tip:

Nuts are much better and easier to digest if you soak them overnight in fresh water with a tablespoon of sea salt. Dry, then bake for a whole day (10-12 hours) at 60°c in the oven.

This makes activates the nutrients – and also makes them very tasty.

The fabulous
BAKER GIRL

Adilia Frazao's Norfolk St Bakery offers up the perfect blend of
English charm and Portuguese passion.

Adilia Frazao can't remember a time when she didn't bake…

Growing up in a tiny village in Portugal, baking was incredibly important in the community. Every Saturday, she'd get together with her mum and grandmother and spend hour upon hour baking for the week ahead. It was half necessity and half a fantastic family bonding time.

Later moving to London to study a degree in hospitality, six years working in pâtisserie environments further added to her already extensive knowledge, before she landed in Cambridge having spotted a listing online for the then shuttered old bakery.

The Norfolk St Bakery itself holds a proud history. Established in 1868, it fed the rapidly growing neighbourhood which sprang up after the railroad came to Cambridge.

Now, under the expert watch of Adilia, it offers a huge range of British and Portuguese artisanal treats.

With white walls, natural woods, original fireplaces and the homely draw of freshly baked goodies, Norfolk St Bakery offers a warming retreat.

Everything from lamb and harissa sausage rolls, to Chelsea buns, to three cheese breads and beyond are on offer, along with great coffee and sandwiches. Then there's the pièce de résistance – the Portuguese custard tarts (be quick though, they tend to sell out within minutes of coming out of the oven).

If you're after brilliant baked goodies, created by a true master of their craft, The Norfolk St Bakery should be your first port of call…

Norfolk Street Bakery
BLUEBERRY CAKE

At home we have a tradition of convent desserts, which are based on egg yolks and almonds. This was the inspiration behind the blueberry and almond cake we serve at Norfolk Street Bakery. Combining the best of both countries, we use the finest blueberries from England and delicious almonds from our homeland, Portugal.

Ingredients

250g butter

250g sugar

5 eggs

200g plain flour

100g ground almonds

100ml sour cream

1 tsp baking powder

150g fresh blueberries

50g flaked almonds

Icing sugar for dusting

Method

Preheat the oven to 180°c.

Grease a round cake tin with a hole in the middle. If you don't have this kind of tin you can used a round one.

Put the butter and the sugar in a bowl with an electric whisk attachment. Whisk on low speed until pale and creamy.

Add the eggs one at a time, making sure they are completely incorporated before adding more.

Add the sour cream, flour, baking powder and almonds until well combined.

Add the blueberries at the end.

Using a rubber spatula, scoop the mixture into the prepared tin.

Bake for 50 minutes to 1 hour, or until a skewer comes out clean when inserted into the centre of the cake.

Remove from the oven and turn out onto a wire rack to cool completely.

When cool, decorate with fresh blueberries some flaked almonds and icing sugar.

The OOO FACTOR

A family affair through and through,
The OOO Company offers Cyprus sunshine in a bottle.

Providing a true taste of Mediterranean sunshine all year round, The OOO Company is the brainchild of couple Rob Marsden and Pam Pantazi whose story reads like something of a fairy-tale.

Rob first fell in love with Cyprus when he lived there in the 1990s. Who knew that, years later, he'd meet his beautiful Cypriot partner, in Cambridge of all places.

Welcomed into the heart of the family, and treated to barbecues and mezes in the glorious Cyprus sunshine, he soon discovered that olive farming was in the blood – and he could get his hands on the best in the business. Deciding to share his secret with the world, The OOO Company was born.

Standing for Original Olive Oil (it's also the sound you make when you try it) what sets The OOO Company apart is the fact that everything comes directly from the makers. There's no middle man – and there never will be.

Natural, healthy and 100% awesome for you, the cold pressed unfiltered oil is produced on the family farm, where the temperature and warm sea breeze offers perfect growing conditions.

While the olives are picked and pressed in the village before being sent to the UK. You can't get the 'Cyprus' olive anywhere outside of Cyprus – which is why OOO's olive oil tastes so wonderfully unique.

Latest products include fantastic flavoured oils (basil, garlic, chilli), flavoured olives (coriander, oregano, garlic, chilli, mixed green and black, stuffed with halloumi) and village style halloumi cheese made in the truly traditional way, of course.

Arguably the best kept secret in the olive oil industry, put a little OOO in your life. You'll be thankful you did…

The OOO Company
THAT CHICKEN & OLIVE THING

Serves 4-6 people.

Ingredients

8 boneless, skinless chicken thigh fillets

12 rashers smoked back bacon, cut roughly into pieces

3 tbsp OOO Company olive oil

1 tbsp dried oregano

3 cloves garlic, crushed

Black pepper, for seasoning

150ml white wine

1 large leek, sliced

2 red peppers, roughly chopped

1 yellow or orange pepper, roughly chopped

250g OOO Company olives

For the halloumi croutons:

150g OOO Company halloumi cheese, cubed

3 tbsp OOO Company olive oil

Method

Preheat the oven to 200^{0}c.

In a deep ovenproof dish, place the chicken pieces, bacon, black pepper, garlic, oregano and OOO Company olive oil. Mix well and place uncovered into the centre of the oven for 20 minutes.

Add the wine, stir well and return to the oven for 10 more minutes.

Add the leek, peppers and olives, stir well and return to the oven for 20 more minutes.

Meanwhile, make the halloumi croutons: heat the oil on a medium to high heat in a shallow pan. Add the diced halloumi and stir regularly (to avoid the cheese burning) until the cheese is golden all over. Then add to the chicken for the last 5 minutes of the cooking time.

Serve with rice. Our tip is to sauté chopped tomatoes, onions and dried oregano in some OOO Company olive oil before adding rice and some chicken stock. This will make lovely flavoured rice which will complement the dish.

Open up
YOUR DOOR

The Pantry isn't so much deli and restaurant; it's something of a stage,
where quality local produce is the star of the show...

Based in Newmarket, this charming establishment is run by husband and wife team Vincent and Anne-Marie, who've gone above and beyond to track down the best suppliers.

From award-winning cheeses courtesy of Mrs Temples of Norfolk, to fine meats from Lane Farm in Brundish (who breed and rear their own rare breed pigs), and even tasty tipples via Dullingham's The English Spirit Company, The Pantry is an Aladdin's cave of regional wonder.

Elsewhere you'll find olives, anti-pasti, artisan breads, jams, marmalades, chutneys and so much more.

The restaurant, with its wonderful open kitchen, serves traditional British food using the plethora of products at hand. The 9oz rib eye steak and Vince's triple chocolate brownie becoming firm favourites with their loyal customers. Working closely with neighbours, Eric Tennant's butchers and Fish! of Burwell, they keep things as fresh and as seasonal as possible – whilst an ever changing, inventive specials board always offers up something new and exciting.

At the deli counter, you'll find made to order sandwiches and salads, soups, quiches, sausage rolls and Scotch eggs – along with fab homemade cakes from their in house baker Jess.

What truly sets The Pantry apart from its peers though is the personal touch. Love their homemade piccalilli? They'll put some in a pot for you. Need a main course for unexpected guests? They'll make up a fish pie, lamb tagine or even a Thai curry to suit your needs. Can't find that elusive ingredient? They'll work with suppliers to try and source it for you.

In addition, when it comes to world produce, they still use local importers and businesses to support the regional industry and keep food miles down.

In the evening, The Pantry transforms from a lively bustling café, into a cosy bistro-style restaurant with a wine and cocktail bar. The menu is enhanced with dishes to suit the chic evening dining experience.

There's a whole lot to discover behind this Pantry door...

The Pantry
BRAWN – PIG'S HEAD TERRINE

Here at The Pantry, we love to dig out old forgotten recipes and at the same time make use of economical cuts of meat. It is good to get to know your local butcher as they can really help with selecting meat cuts. A good butcher will also help with cooking suggestions.

Brawn is traditional recipe of pig's head set in its own jelly; now this description and handling the actual preparation may put a lot of people off, but I think the meat when cooked slowly is fantastic and beats pork loin or chops hands down in the flavour department.

There is a lot of meat available on a pig's head, from the tongue to the cheeks and even the ears. A pig's head won't cost you much at all and will easily give you 10 generous portions of pâté which is great served with toasted bread and cornichons.

The recipe is quite time consuming – but much of this is the simmering of the pig's head while you can potter on with other things.

Ingredients

1 pig's head

1 large onion

1 large leek

1 large carrot

10 peppercorns

1 tsp coriander seeds

2 bay leaves

2 pig's trotters (optional)

2 bulbs garlic

Bunch chopped parsley

Bunch parsley stalks

Method

The butcher should have already prepared the pig's head for you. If not then you can quite easily get to grips with any remaining hairs with a disposable razor.

The pig's head needs to be first brought up to the boil to ensure any impurities are removed. Place the pig's head in a large stock pot and cover with cold water and bring to the boil, (if using trotters add them at this stage).

Once this is done change the water and start again. This time adding all the vegetables and the herbs and spices.

Once the water is boiling, drop the heat to a gentle simmer – you should never boil meat that you intend to eat as it will become tough – a gentle simmer is all that is needed. The simmering will also allow you to skim off any impurities which will rise to the surface while cooking. The pig's head now needs to simmer until the flesh is giving and soft, this is anywhere between 3-5 hours, depending on the size of the pig's head.

Once cooked take off the heat and let the pig's head cool in the stock slightly.

Remove from the stock and strain the liquid to a fresh saucepan. This can be reduced further if needed.

When cool enough to handle, take all of the meat off the head and retain some of the fat to put through the brawn (optional).

Take the skin off the tongue and chop up with a knife. Add to the rest of the meat.

Check the seasoning of the meat; remember that when cold, the seasoning will be less intense. Then add some chopped parsley and a couple of ladles of the reduced stock, push into a terrine, individual ramekins or a traditional bowl shaped vessel. Top up with the stock and chill.

To serve, enjoy with sourdough, piccalilli, and make further use of your pig's head by crisping up the ears and adding some texture.

Tip: The remaining stock is fantastic in soups like pea and ham or minestrone.

All hail
THE ALE

Meat. Bread. Beer. That's the Pint Shop's motto
but they don't just stop there...

Inspired by the beer houses of the 1830s, the Pint Shop is a hark back to simpler times.

See, back in the day, beer was originally a rich man's drink due to its high tax, with the poor having to make do with copious amounts of gin to make it through the day.

All that changed in 1830 when the beer act was passed meaning folks could then brew and sell their own beer from home. The beer house was born and so was the next generation of beer drinkers.

The Pint Shop captures the essence of this era, offering a welcoming, down-to-earth place where people of all walks of life can gather to enjoy brilliant beer and simple British food cooked over hot charcoal.

They embrace drinking and eating equally with 16 craft beers on tap (mostly British, all from small brewers), 80 gins (including their very own 'one-of-a-kind' blend 'P' made using peas as the lead botanical) and wines from small European growers alongside an array of barbecued treats.

From smoked beef dripping and garlic toast to nibble on, to potted brisket, pickled walnuts, parsley and toast to start, through to overnight pork belly, flageolet beans and bacon for the main event – the list goes on and will simply have you salivating. What's more, the menus represent fantastic value for money and their Sunday roasts are truly epic.

Be it a beer, light lunch or a full on banquet, the Pint Shop combines ye olde charm with modern day magic to create a winning formula that'll keep you coming back for more...

SET MENU (Available 12noon-7pm Monday-Friday)

PINT·SHOP

STARTERS
Caesar Salad
Devilled Mackerel, Fennel & Orange
Grilled Asparagus, Brown Butter Mayo, Poached Egg

MAINS
Pork & Apple Burger, Bacon Jam, Applewood
Grilled Salmon, Cauliflower Rice
Stichelton, Watercress, Walnut & Pea Salad

PUDDINGS
Coffee Parfait, Biscotti
Apples & Oats
Stichelton, Chutney, Fruit Bread

TWO COURSES £10 THREE COURSES £13

10 Peas Hill, Cambridge CB2 3PN

PINT SHOP GARDEN OPEN

← BAR
DINING ROOM →

PINT·SHOP
MEAT. BREAD. BEER.

Pint Shop
#1

This is our version of a British classic. It's perfect for barbecues with friends or lazy evenings in the garden. Here we're using strawberries, but it works equally well with other soft berries.

Ingredients

For the strawberry gin base spirit:

250g fresh strawberries

1 bottle gin. We use Adnams Copper House, but any bold juniper gin will work well.

For the Pint Shop No.1:

20ml strawberry infused gin

20ml Lillet sweet vermouth

10ml triple sec

125ml dry ginger ale (if you like things a little sweeter, use lemonade)

Orange peel

1 slice cucumber

3 fresh mint leaves

Method

First you need to make the base spirit. This takes a couple of days, so needs to be planned ahead. Make a full bottle as it keeps well for at least a couple of months.

Wash and halve the strawberries, put them in a one litre kilner jar. Add the gin (keeping the empty bottle) and leave for 36-48 hours depending on the ripeness and redness of strawberries.

Sieve the infused gin back into the bottle.

Keep the gin infused strawberries – you can serve them with jelly and ice cream for a boozy kick or freeze them and use them to garnish the finished drink.

To make the Pint Shop No.1 cocktail, combine all of the ingredients in a tall glass with lots of ice and stir gently.

Pint Shop
LAMB, PEAS & BREAD

Serves 6 as starter or light dinner,
with plenty of lamb left over for a mid-week dinner.

Ingredients

For the lamb:

1 tbsp coriander seeds

1 tsp cumin seeds

3 tbsp rapeseed oil

1 (1.5kg) spring lamb shoulder on the bone

1 leek, cut into 3cm pieces

2 sticks celery, cut into 3cm pieces

7 shallots, cut in half

4 bay leaves

6 sprigs rosemary

1.5 litres chicken stock

¼ nutmeg

Maldon salt and black pepper, for seasoning

For the rest:

500g peas, fresh or frozen

75g butter

2 shallots, cut into rings

1 small handful pea shoots/watercress

Berkswell or Pecorino cheese, to grate over the dish

1 lemon, zest only

1 tbsp olive oil, for the bread

Sourdough, 1 slice per person and a few more for seconds

Method

For the lamb

Preheat the oven to 120°c and heat a heavy based casserole pan (it needs a lid) on a medium heat.

Season the lamb and toast the coriander and cumin seeds and then roughly grind them with a pestle and mortar.

Add the rapeseed oil to the pan and turn to a medium to high heat. Add the lamb and brown on all sides, then remove and set aside.

Add the vegetables, bay leaves and rosemary, then brown off. Once tender, and they have taken on some colour, add the ground spices and cook for 1 minute until the aroma hits your nose.

Now put the lamb back and add the chicken stock and bring to a simmer. Cover with a disc of greaseproof paper and pop the lid on and place in the oven.

Cook for 3-4 hours, until the meat will easily pull away from the bone.

Remove from the oven and leave to cool until you can comfortably handle the meat. Take the meat and strain the vegetables and herbs (discard the rosemary stalks) and keep the liquor.

Place the liquor back on the burner on a high heat and reduce by two thirds, season with nutmeg, salt and pepper. Skim the fat off as you go.

Pick the meat off the bone into 4-5cm pieces, removing any fat and sinew. Place back into the liquor along with vegetables.

If you have time, it's best left to mature overnight in the fridge.

For the peas

Heat the butter in a heavy based saucepan and add the shallots with a sprinkling of Maldon salt. Sauté until tender and translucent.

Place the peas into food processor and blitz to a coarse chop.

Once the shallots are soft, add the peas and season.

They are now ready for serving.

To serve, warm the lamb up in the oven at 140°c, until hot.

Toast the olive oil brushed sourdough, ideally on a griddle pan.

Spread on the peas and pile on the lamb.

Grate the Berkswell and scatter the lemon zest and pea shoots over the dish.

Prince CHARMING

For a proper boozer full of barroom banter, alongside a stylish restaurant, you'd be hard pressed to do better than The Prince Albert…

Part of a 'holy trinity' pub family, which also consists of The Anchor Inn and The Royal Standard. The Prince Albert offers an unpretentious environment in which to enjoy a quality pint and flavoursome fare.

Based in Ely, they pride themselves on being the area's 'proper pub', with a back-to-basics attitude, there's no music, TV or gaming machines – in fact nothing to distract from what it's all actually about… food, drink, and friendly banter.

Traditionally a backstreet boozer for locals (and prior to that the officer's mess for the local militia), 2014 saw a major refurbishment to create the venue's stylish dining area. It was a smart move which allowed for those who just wanted a drink to do so in the manner they'd become accustomed.

A 2015 CAMRA 'Pub of the Year', the beer here is as good as it gets – with ten hand pumps on offer serving well-kept real ales. The menu, meanwhile, features an array of local fresh produce, such as Fenland celery, Denham estate meats and new season fenland carrots and creative dishes like pan fried chicken supreme with sag aloo, curried butternut squash purée, puy lentils and coconut sauce and pan fried hake with herbed dauphinoise potatoes, sofrito sauce, samphire, braised shallots and balsamic purée – the burgers here are legendary too.

What's more, The Prince Albert is also home to Ely's biggest beer garden…

Be it fun in the sun, a cheery chat or fine food and drink, this traditional gem will ensure you enjoy it all without any distractions…

The Prince Albert

STRAWBERRY & CREAM DELICE

With rhubarb sorbet and macaroon.

Ingredients

For the strawberry and cream delice:

500g strawberry purée

250g caster sugar

13 gelatine leaves

900ml double cream

250g egg whites

For the macaroons:

90g egg whites

125g icing sugar

125g ground almonds

Red food dye

2 tbsp water

110g caster sugar

For the rhubarb sorbet:

500ml rhubarb purée

500ml stock syrup

50g glucose

Method

For the strawberry and cream delice

Boil strawberry purée with 250g of caster sugar and nine of the gelatine leaves, then allow to cool.

Lightly whip 500ml of double cream, fold this cream into the cooled strawberry purée.

Lightly whip the egg whites, fold this into the mix and then allow to set in a container.

Boil the remaining double cream and add the remaining gelatine leaves, then allow to cool.

Pour the cooled mixture onto the set strawberry delice (if the mixture is too warm it will melt the delice and all blend in together.

Allow time to set.

For the macaroons

Make a paste with the icing sugar, ground almonds and 40g of the egg whites.

Boil the caster sugar, water and a few drops of food dye to 115°c.

Whip the remaining egg whites and pour the boiled sugar mixture over, whilst whisking.

Fold egg mix into the almond paste gently.

Pipe mix onto a tray and stand for 20 minutes.

Bake for 10-15 minutes on 160°c.

Make a basic butter icing and use to sandwich between two macaroons.

For the rhubarb sorbet

Boil the rhubarb purée, stock syrup and glucose altogether on a stove.

Add this mixture to an ice-cream machine and churn.

Place mixture in freezer to solidify.

The LION KING

For a right royal welcome, The Red Lion Inn Hinxton takes pride of place.

Holding court in the heart of the quaint conservation village of Hinxton since the 16th century, the multi award-winning Red Lion Inn is a privately owned free house pub/restaurant complete with bed and breakfast accommodation.

Housed in a historic Grade II listed building, exposed beams, warming fires and Chesterfield sofas welcome you as you step through the doors and essentially back in time.

In warmer climes, the inn's quintessentially English walled garden (created by local garden designer Ian Shooter, a Chelsea Flower Show award-winner) provides a tranquil retreat under the watchful gaze of the dovecote and village church watchtower – whilst a striking oak extension offers a spacious and elegant room for dining fit for royalty.

Classic British dishes are the order of the day here lovingly created with finesse using only the freshest, locally sourced, produce. Everything from smoked Denham Estate venison loin with watercress, pecan and pear salad and redcurrant coulis, to sole and wild mushroom bouchées with roasted truffle potatoes, sautéed pak choi and red chilli is on offer.

It's award-winning food too, boasting an AA rosette. The menus change with the availability of fresh produce and the changing seasons, meaning the 'Specials Board' is always worth a gander.

Eight stunning guest rooms were awarded four AA stars and designed by local architect Rosalind Bird, are discreetly positioned in the grounds, located in the delightful private garden. What's more, each room has been named after a local beer or cider producer (think Nelson's Revenge and Old Speckled Hen).

Offering effortless elegance, and oodles of charm, The Red Lion Inn, Hinxton, is undoubtedly the king of its jungle…

FREE HOUSE

HINXTON

HINXTON

Photo: Joanna Randall

THE
RED LION
INN · HINXTON

Photo: Joanna Randall

Black Bull & Red Lion
POPPY SEED CRUSTED FILLET OF VENISON

With pomegranate reduction, Jerusalem artichoke purée, kohlrabi and beetroot.

Ingredients

For the fillet of venison:

200g venison fillet

3 tbsp poppy seeds

2 tbsp maple syrup

4 cloves

Vegetable oil

Butter

For the pomegranate reduction:

1 onion, sliced

1 carrot, sliced

1 celery stick, sliced

3 black peppercorns

5 juniper berries

2 bay leaves

200g venison trim

Water, to cover

30-50ml pomegranate molasses

2 tbsp honey

3 cloves

Salt for seasoning

For the Jerusalem artichoke purée:

300g Jerusalem artichoke

Boiling water, to cover

50ml double cream

Salt and white pepper

For Kohlrabi mustard vinaigrette:

1 tsp wholegrain mustard

1 tsp honey

30ml white wine vinegar

60ml olive oil

Salt

1 kohlrabi, peeled and thinly sliced

For the beetroot:

1 beetroot, thinly sliced

2 tbsp vegetable oil

To garnish:

Pomegranate seeds

Chives, finely sliced

Beetroot cubes

Method

For the venison

Trim and remove any sinew on the venison, seal in a hot pan with vegetable oil and a little butter until nicely coloured. In a mixing bowl, coat the venison in maple syrup and then add the cloves by crushing the buds, followed by the poppy seeds. Transfer to a baking tray and cook at 180°c for 9-12 minutes. Rest for half the cooking time, slice on the angle and serve.

For the pomegranate reduction

Colour the venison trim in the oven for 30-45 minutes at 180°c. Place all the ingredients in a saucepan except for the cloves, honey and pomegranate molasses. Bring to the boil and then reduce to a low simmer for 2-3 hours. Strain the stock through a fine sieve and place in a fresh pan, add the pomegranate molasses and honey then reduce slowly to a syrup consistency. This should take around 30 minutes. Finish by crushing the clove buds into the sauce.

For the Jerusalem artichoke purée

Quickly peel and thinly slice the artichoke into enough water to cover, add the cream and season. Bring to a simmer and cook until the artichoke is tender. Remove the artichoke from the pan and blitz in a blender, adding some of the cooking liquor until the right consistency is reached. Pass through a fine sieve.

For the kohlrabi

First make the vinaigrette by combining all the ingredients minus the kohlrabi. Peel and thinly slice the kohlrabi making sure it's completely covered in the vinaigrette and marinate for 30 minutes.

For the beetroot

Thinly slice the beetroot and pan fry in the vegetable oil for 2-3 minutes, turning frequently. Pat off excess oil before serving.

Assemble all the elements on the plate and add the garnish and sauce last.

Setting THE STANDARD

With historical roots, but a modern outlook, The Royal Standard offers a game of two halves when it comes to drinking and dining…

The oldest building on Ely's Fore Hill, just off the Market Square, The Royal Standard started as a one room public house way back in the 15th century.

Today specialising in steak and seafood, it's been extended and lovingly refurbished over the years to bring the historical building in line with the modern world – ultimately becoming one of the area's most popular hangouts.

Offering a relaxed atmosphere and first-class service, inside you'll find a spacious dining area and a well-stocked bar featuring well-maintained real ales, premium spirits, expertly prepared cocktails and 60 wines by the bottle – whilst outside awaits their gorgeous terrace for al fresco drinking and dining.

The food menu is extensive with a strong focus on grilled, fresh, locally-sourced seasonal produce. Traditional pub favourites are always available but you'll also find plenty of thinking outside the box, like tempura salt and pepper squid with pickled vegetables and sweet chilli sauce to start and scallop, sea trout, chorizo and chimichuri skewers for your main – whilst from the grill you can get everything from a 16oz T-bone steak right through to a 20oz rib eye or a simple grilled tuna steak – not forgetting their ever popular 'Friday Steak Night'.

Every month there are live events, such as 'Dinner with Jazz' on the first Thursday of the month, making this a lively location which appeals to drinkers and diners across the board.

Consistently moving forward, The Royal Standard is the perfect combination of old meets new, where you'll receive a friendly welcome as standard.

The Royal Standard
SOFT SHELL CRAB

With warm oriental salad. Serves 4.

Ingredients

4 soft shell crabs

For the crab breadcrumb:

200g polenta

1 tbsp flour

1 tsp curry powder

1 tsp five spice powder

Oil for frying

For the salad:

1 leek

1 shallot

2 carrots

1 chilli

200g pak choi

For the sauce:

1 orange

1 clove roasted garlic

2 tbsp honey

100ml soy sauce

Method

For the crab

Mix all the ingredients together and set aside until ready.

Coat the crabs evenly in the breadcrumbs and fry in oil until golden brown.

For the salad & sauce

Cut all the vegetables into fine thin strips and fry lightly in a hot pan.

In a separate pan, add the juice of the orange along with the roasted garlic, honey and soy sauce. Reduce the sauce until desired consistency then strain.

Add the sauce to the vegetables then turn out onto plates.

Place on top of the plated oriental salad and serve.

A passion
FOR PIGS

Annabel and Andrew Sedgwick's foodie journey began with the
ultimate romantic Christmas present – a sausage stuffer.
This was the seed from which Sedgwick's Charcuterie was born...

Initially purchasing pork from friends, and inspired by many a Mediterranean holiday, the Sedgwicks' experimented with making their own charcuterie, air dried hams, chorizos and salamis.

In 2013, they made the brave decision to quit their day jobs and move to their smallholding in Cambridgeshire. They took the step to rear more pigs on their land, convert their outbuilding into a butchery, grow their own vegetables, and rear chickens, ducks and guinea fowl for their eggs and meat.

Following further tasting trips to Europe, including a week touring the Artisan Norcini (pork butchers) of Tuscany, they took the step to convert their outbuilding into a butchery and recreate the conditions of an Italian curing cellar so they could make and sell their own charcuterie. They launched Sedgwick's Charcuterie in 2014 and haven't looked back!

Having developed recipes and methods of curing to make a mouth-watering selection of their own salamis, chorizos and cured, air-dried meats they have a growing customer base at both St Ives and Ely farmers markets, as well as online.

Provenance is key here; many of the herbs used for flavourings are fresh from their gardens, the cider in the salami is often made using their own apples and the honey in the cures is from their own bees.

What's more, their rare-breed pigs are all 100% free range and live in either meadow paddocks or small areas of native woodland – with plenty of fresh forage.

Combining British traditions and flavours with that of the continent, along with a passion for local produce, Sedgwick's Charcuterie is a true stamp of great taste and quality.

Sedgwick's Charcuterie
SOBRASSADA CHICKEN

With cannellini beans.

This recipe is based on a traditional Majorcan recipe, where they may also use rabbit; it's also great with fish. Serves 4.

Sobrassada is a soft textured, spreadable chorizo, typical of the Balearic Islands and southern Spain native to the island of Majorca. Our rare breed sobrassada is slow matured for a rich full flavour. It has a creamy texture and a sweet, soft, smoky taste to balance the spice. It's great simply spread on bread, with a drizzle of honey, but it's also a wonderfully versatile cooking ingredient. It's fantastic on a pizza, in a pasta sauce or risotto, as a base for a beef casserole or cooked with fish. It also transforms a roast chicken if spread generously under the skin.

Ingredients

For the tomato sauce:

1 medium onion diced

2 cloves garlic, finely sliced

600g tomatoes, fresh or tinned

For the main dish:

4 free range chicken breasts, skin on

200g Sedgwick's Charcuterie rare breed sobrassada

Small glass white wine

100g dried canellini beans soaked overnight or 1 x 400g can of cannellini beans drained and rinsed

2 tablespoons olive oil

Salt and black pepper

A handful of flat leaf parsley

Method

If using soaked dried beans, cover with water in a pan, bring to the boil and simmer for 30 minutes or until tender. Drain and set aside.

Start by making your tomato sauce, gently fry the onion until translucent, add the garlic and continue to fry for a couple of minutes. Add the tomatoes, a little salt and pepper and leave to simmer on a medium heat for 20 minutes.

Season your chicken breasts, add some olive oil to a hot frying pan and fry the chicken, skin side down for 5 minutes until golden brown. Turn them over and fry for a further 5 minutes.

Turn the heat down to medium and add the sobrassada, give it time to gently melt, add the glass of white wine and mix well. Baste the chicken breasts with the sauce, cover and allow to simmer for 20 minutes. Every few minutes, baste the chicken with more of the sauce to allow the flavour to infuse the chicken and to keep it moist.

Uncover the pan, add the tomatoes and beans, stir well and leave to simmer for 5 minutes. Serve with seasonal green veg (we've used asparagus from the garden), some crusty bread and sprinkle over the chopped parsley.

From the SHELF

If you've ever visited Shelford Delicatessen, you'll have seen, smelled and tasted the passion in what they do...

Shelford Delicatessen is an independent kitchen, deli and café established by Drew and Nikki Wilkinson whom, upon returning home to England in 1999, noticed a distinct lack of ingredients and food creativity on the UK high street.

Back then, it was hard to even buy modern day staples such as chorizo, and so the challenge was set. Shelford Delicatessen was launched with the simple idea of sourcing only the best sustainable ingredients and cooking with them.

The business has developed its own style of rustic, café-restaurant foods made with care and respect, to produce wonderful homemade breakfasts, lunches and dinners. These you can eat in, take out or order for an event.

Besides casseroles, lasagnes, tagines and fishcakes, this place makes everything from lush green pesto, pastes and smoky chorizo jam, through to seasonal salads, ice cream, gorgeous cakes and fruit preserves. The shop itself specialises in artisan products aiming to ensure that guests go away with the whole experience of how a product goes from grower to shelf.

It's grown from a once tiny shop into a large attractive lunch venue that nestles in the friendly, leafy community of Great Shelford. The plain stone floors and wooden tables in the airy deli café and secluded garden are the perfect backdrop for wholesome dishes and seriously good coffee.

The lovely team are passionate about good food, fab coffee and great customer service. You can watch baristas at work, chefs discussing ingredients and meet friendly staff at the lunch counter full of fresh daily specials – all made in the kitchens at the heart of the shop.

These are just a few reasons why this deli has been voted one of The Independent's top 50 deli's in the UK.

Photo credit: Fanny Bara

Shelford Delicatessen

Shelford Deli
ASPARAGUS WITH MANCHEGO & PIMENTON

Ingredients

2 bunches asparagus

Manchego cheese

Pimenton de le Vera, Spanish smoked paprika

Extra virgin olive oil

Salt and pepper to season

Method

Blanch two bunches of asparagus in boiling water for approximately 2 minutes until just soft enough to eat but not breaking. Alternatively, slice courgettes lengthways, but do not blanch.

Chargrill on griddle plate, or barbecue, alternatively char under the grill.

When still hot put onto plates and top with the Manchego cheese. Buy the best you can find. Slice very finely so it melts easily.

Dust with Pimenton de la Vera (Spanish smoked paprika).

Drizzle liberally with good extra virgin olive oil.

Add sea salt and black pepper to serve.

PANZANELLA

For the bread:

6 thick slices of old bread, cut into 2cm cubes

Olive oil, plenty needed to soak bread, this will also be part of the dressing.

2 cloves garlic, cut into four

For the salad:

4 peppers

8 ripe tomatoes cut into small chunks

1 clove of garlic very finely chopped, then a ½ tsp of salt poured over the top and mashed again

1 red onion, very finely sliced

1 tbsp capers

1 bunch basil

15 black olives

1-2 handfuls rocket leaves

5 tbsp white wine vinegar

100g fresh salad leaves

Extra virgin olive oil to finish

Select your bread; we like to use a sourdough from our wonderful local Dovcote Bakery, here in Cambridge.

Toss breadcubes and garlic in olive oil. Cook at 180°c until really crisp and golden then set aside to cool.

In a large bowl, mix together the onion and salted garlic and leave for 20 minutes.

Add in tomatoes, capers, olives and half the basil. Toss and set aside for an hour.

Cut the peppers cut into 8, toss in oil and sea salt and roast in a tray in the oven until soft and velvety, then chop up.

Mix in chopped peppers and vinegar.

Add in cooled bread cubes and basil (keep a few sprigs for garnish) and let it sit for a few minutes. Check seasoning.

Finally layer salad leaves, rocket and panzanella into serving bowl. Drizzle with extra virgin olive oil to serve.

Shelford Deli
SLOW ROAST LAMB

With Manzanilla sherry and spinach.

Ingredients

1 shoulder of good quality free-range lamb, seasoned

6 tbsp olive oil

Half bottle of white wine

1 tsp cumin seeds

1 tsp coriander seeds

5 allspice berries

25 black peppercorns

8 bay leaves

1 tsp sea salt

1 onion cut into 6

1 bulb garlic cut in half, broken up

4 carrots peeled, cut into 6

200ml Manzanilla sherry

400g fresh young spinach washed, chopped roughly

Extra virgin olive oil to finish

Method

Buy the best lamb shoulder you can afford; we always use Barker Bros Butchers for their excellent free-range lamb.

Heat olive oil until hot, brown the lamb on all sides.

Rub in all ingredients except sherry and spinach, cover and place in oven for minimum of 4 hours at 160°c-180°c (better all day at 140°c) until meat falls apart when pushed. Drain juices off and keep, cover lamb and set aside.

Let juices settle, scoop off fat (save for birds), pour juices back into a pan with Manzanilla sherry and cook until glossy and a little sticky (reduce to third of the volume).

Add spinach, we use Wild Country Organics because it tastes homegrown.

Cook spinach quickly in the juices. Check seasoning, it needs to be strong and a little salty as it has to season all the lamb.

Pull bones out of lamb and break into pieces (it will fall apart.) Pour juices and spinach on top, arrange to look beautiful and finish with extra virgin olive oil to serve. We don't serve this too hot, the flavours work best below 70°c.

RHUBARB, ORANGE & ALMOND POLENTA CAKE

You could also try this recipe with pears or any other soft fruit.

For the rhubarb:

4 sticks rhubarb, cut into bite sized pieces

100g sugar

Juice of 1 orange and 1 lemon

Zest of 1 orange and 1 lemon

2 star anise

2 cloves

1 vanilla pod, split lengthways

100g honey

For the cake:

200g unsalted butter

200g caster sugar

300g ground almonds

1 vanilla pod, seeds

3 eggs

Zest of 1 lemon and 1 orange

1 tsp orange blossom water, or a little orange juice

120g polenta flour

1 tsp baking powder

In a saucepan, cook the rhubarb and the other ingredients on a gentle heat until soft but not falling apart.

Grease and line a 10" cake tin, arrange the rhubarb in the bottom and pour over the juices.

Scrape the seeds out of the vanilla pod and add to sugar. Beat butter, sugar and zests together until pale and creamy.

Slowly add the eggs, beating well in between each one.

Add the polenta, ground almonds, orange blossom water and baking powder and mix well.

Spoon the mix over the rhubarb and bake at 160°c for 45 minutes.

Allow to cool and turn out onto a board.

Let them EAT CAKE...

Tom Dolby is a master baker – and Tom's Cakes are the business...

Tom Dolby is from a long line of bakers with his family opening their first bakery in 1803.

Beginning his training in the family business, Tom quickly realised there was a big wide world of baking out there, so to further develop his knowledge and skills, he began to work as a freelance baker.

His travels took him as far afield as Australia and New Zealand and, having worked in a number of leading bakeries both overseas and in the UK, he took the plunge to set up his own business with a focus on seasonality – an approach relatively unusual in baking.

After a number of years trading on farmers' markets, and supplying farm shops, in 2014 Tom's Cakes opened its first café and shop in St Ives.

Every single cake and biscuit they sell is hand-made in their Cambridgeshire bakery. Baked in small batches, they don't use any mixes, everything is made from scratch using natural ingredients under the careful supervision of Tom.

Their eggs are free-range from local farms, the flour is milled in Essex and the vegetables are from the Fens. In season, the fruit is from local farmers, and their lavender is from Norfolk. At Tom's, they take the provenance of their ingredients extremely seriously.

Tom's café and shop is located in the historic former Toll House at 19 Market Hill, St Ives. Having sat empty for many years, the restoration project was a lengthy one, but they've sensitively restored and adapted the Grade II listed building to allow customers the opportunity both to buy cakes and biscuits to take home or to enjoy in the company of friends in the shop, with a delicious cup of coffee or tea.

Tom's Cakes
GINGER CAKE

Ingredients

For the cake:

220ml golden syrup

220ml treacle

220g brown sugar

560ml milk

460g self-raising flour

220g unsalted butter, softened

2 eggs

100g stem ginger in syrup, drained and grated

2tsp bicarbonate of soda

2tsp cinnamon

2tsp mixed spice

2tbsp ground ginger

For the frosting:

125g butter

250g icing sugar

125g cream cheese

4 pieces stem ginger in syrup, chopped

1 un-waxed lemon, zest

Method

Sift together the self-raising flour, bicarbonate of soda, cinnamon, mixed spice and ground ginger in a large mixing bowl. Add the butter and rub together to make fine breadcrumbs.

Heat the milk, treacle, syrup and brown sugar in a pan on a medium heat, stirring continuously until fully blended together.

Add this a little at a time to the breadcrumb mix ensuring it's well combined.

Mix the eggs and the grated stem ginger together and add to the mixture.

Grease and line a 10" cake tin. Pour in the cake mix.

Bake for 1 hour and 10 minutes at 160˚c.

For the frosting

Use an electric hand whisk to mix together the butter, icing sugar and cream cheese until fluffy. Using a palette knife spread the frosting on top of the cake. Scatter the chopped pieces of sweetened stem ginger over the frosting.

Before serving, sprinkle with the zest of a lemon.

Shed LOADS

The Urban Shed holds all the tools to create
the ultimate sandwich shop experience...

Situated on King Street in Cambridge is The Urban Shed – a sandwich shop with a difference.

Owner Simon Morrice was pretty much born into the catering industry, and his career prior to opening The Urban Shed makes for impressive reading (highlights include a stint with Raymond Blanc and the running of Jools Holland's jazz club).

He's put his heart and soul into the venture meaning the establishment is a true reflection of himself.

Fusing contemporary, cool and retro furnishings, with a vast vinyl collection which customers can play, buy or trade and a forward way of thinking about food, The Urban Shed has rightly become a popular hangout for the more discerning snacker.

Offering banging breakfasts and groovy shakes amongst other tasty treats, the sandwiches are the real star of the show – inventive concoctions on your choice of fresh bread.

There's everything from sesame shredded pork, spring onion and lemongrass mayo to hoisin duck, pickled cucumber and basil mayo on offer – all using the very finest local ingredients.

With their gluten-free bread option and range of homemade gluten-free deserts, coeliacs are also well looked after at the Shed. Their own Urban blend coffee is the icing on the cake and always check out 'The Shed Test Board' for daily creations.

Here, it's very much a 'Cheers' mentality – sometimes you want to go where everyone knows your name – and it's why The Urban Shed has developed a loyal following. For Simon, it's all about creating that friendly village pub vibe in a sandwich shop setting. Regulars even have their own mug with their name on!

Offering venue hire, a dinner party service and outside catering on the side, The Urban Shed is your home away from home.

Urban Shed guide
TO THE ULTIMATE SHED SANDWICH

The Urban Shed's six step guide to your definitive bread buddy…

1. **The tone!**

   Bang some tunes on! We like to whack out vinyl classics. The retro vibes help enhance creativity.

2. **The foundation.**

   We use a local independent artisan baker, using only organic flour for something that's fresh out of the oven that day. It's a world away from the pre-sliced packaged stuff you'll find in the supermarkets. Using our granary bloomer, ciabatta or even gluten free loaf – envisage your sandwich and start to build your base. It's crucial that only a good quality butter is then used to spread on both sides.

3. **The filling.**

   There's no right or wrong answer here; whether you fancy meat, fish or veggie, we like to mix it up at 'The Shed' and always think outside of the box. For meateaters, we only buy quality meat from our local butcher. From 52°c cooked beef to 8 hour slow-cooked pork belly. Whichever meat you choose, treat it with love.

   For fish lovers, locally smoked or sustainably sourced is key – and for all you veggies, there's so much local seasonal produce you can never fail to create a great veggie sandwich. Everyone loves a bit of cheese, and with loads of amazing local cheese on our doorstep, it'd simply be a crime not to include some. But remember, good cheese doesn't always have to be melted!

4. **The condiment.**

   Our old friend mayo tends to be the go-to buddy – but there are plenty of alternatives. Think mustard, relish, piccalilli, horseradish or, as we sometimes do, try a combination of a couple. If you're feeling adventurous, make your own from scratch, we take a lot of pride in ours.

5. **The garnish.**

   Garnishes are important to sandwiches as they add texture and a new dynamic. We use a varied selection to enhance our creations – from micro-herbs to crackling. Fresh, crisp lettuce is very important, yet often overlooked, so give your garnish as much love as we do!

6. **The end.**

   Your work here is done. Now, time for your reward. Sit back and munch.

P.S. Failing all that, head along to us and we'll do all the hard work for you!

The Bird's
THE WORD...

'There is no love more sincere than the love of food'.
That's the motto at Fordham's The White Pheasant...

Head chef and proprietor Calvin Holland, is the driving force and mastermind behind The White Pheasant's rapid, and much deserved, rise in reputation.

Having initially trained at the Fordham establishment back in 2005, he went on to ply his trade and earn his stripes at a host of the UK's finest multi rosette and Michelin star restaurants – before returning to The Pheasant's familiar shores in 2013 to take over the reins.

Just nine months later and a coveted 2AA rosette award for culinary excellence was in the bag.

Here, it's a winning combo of locally sourced, seasonal produce, exquisitely executed alongside award-winning wines hand-picked by their sommelier.

Specialising in quality ingredients, from local game to freshly caught fish, the cuisine at The White Pheasant looks just as stunning as it tastes. As their motto suggests, Calvin and his team are truly passionate about serving up only the very best.

From shoulder of pork bon bon with burnt apple, cider and pickled salad to start, through to hake with seared scallop, sweetcorn, potato dice and mushroom cream for the main event, every ingredient is carefully considered before being conjured into magic on a plate.

Boasting a wonderful dining setting, with weathered floorboards and warming open fire, their five course seasonal taster menus have also proved to be a popular draw.

The White Pheasant is the very epitome of contemporary country dining. The word about this particular bird is well and truly out...

"The most warmest of welcome's was followed by an absolute "EXPLOSION" of Pure gastronomic delight's!!"
Thank you!
Best wishes
Jeff & Linda Nash.

Sit Long...
Talk Lots...
Laugh often...

the white pheasant

country bar & restaurant

the white pheasant

The White Pheasant
BEETROOT MOUSSE

with pine nuts, whipped goats' cheese, pear and pickles.

Ingredients

For the beetroot mousse:

300g beetroot purée

150g semi-whipped cream

3 egg whites

5 gelatine leaves

½ lemon juice

Pinch of salt

For the whipped goats' cheese:

½ log goats' cheese (500g)

250ml milk

3 gelatine leaves

200g semi-whipped cream

Salt

For the pickling liquor:

200ml water

200ml white wine vinegar

100g sugar

1 cinnamon stick

2 star anise

6 peppercorns

2 sprigs thyme

For the pickled garnish:

2 pears, cut into 1cm dice

2 large purple beetroot, cut into 1cm dice

1 bunch candied beetroot, cooked

200g radish, thinly sliced

Garnish:

200g pine nuts

Rocket cress

Method

For the beetroot mousse

Soak the gelatine leaves in cold water and leave to one side for 5 minutes.

Once the gelatine has softened, squeeze out any excess water and add to the slightly warmed beetroot purée. Whisk until all the gelatine has dissolved. Leave to one side and cool slightly.

Whip the egg whites until a soft peak and then fold through the beetroot purée mix. Once mixed together, add the semi-whipped cream, salt and lemon juice to season.

Place in a cling film lined tray and set for 2 hours before portioning.

For the whipped goats' cheese

Soak the gelatine leaves in cold water. Leave to one side for 5 minutes. Once the gelatine has softened, squeeze out any excess water. Bring the milk to the boil then add the gelatine.

Place the goats' cheese in a food processor, add the milk mix and blend until smooth.

Pass through a fine sieve.

Once chilled, fold in the semi-whipped cream and add seasoning to taste.

Place into a piping bag and chill.

For the pickling liquor

Place all of the ingredients into a pan and bring to the boil. Leave to chill.

For the pickled garnish

Prepare the garnish to be pickled.

Once prepared, place the pickling liquor over the garnish and leave for 24 hours – this will be plenty of time for these to take on the flavour.

Toast the pine nuts, add to pestle and mortar and lightly crush.

To assemble the dish

Take the whipped goats' cheese out of the fridge for 5 minutes to soften slightly.

Cut the beetroot mousse into finger long slices and place onto your chosen plate (in the restaurant we like to use a lot of hand crafted china stoneware crockery).

Drain all the pickled garnishes onto a paper towel and leave for 1 minute (this will stop any of the pickling liquor from running on the plate).

Using your own judgement, place a piece of the pickled garnish next to the beetroot mousse. Next, add small pipings of the whipped goats' cheese, and then more pickled garnish on top – trying to give the dish as much height as possible. To finish, sprinkle the crushed pine nuts and some small sprigs of rocket cress.

Happy EVER AFTER

Offering a fairy tale setting, a visit to The Willow Tree is a truly enchanting drinking and dining experience...

Set within the picturesque village of Bourn, The Willow Tree is a family business owned and loved by husband and wife team Craig and Shaina Galvin-Scott.

Originally from Liverpool, Shaina has a background in TV, events and interior design, whilst Craig has been a chef since the day his lovely Nanny Lilly taught him to cook – plying his trade across Cornwall, London and France prior to Cambridgeshire.

Since opening The Willow Tree in 2009, they've not only enjoyed success and national acclaim, they've also brought beautiful twin girls Bo and Fifi into their very full and happy world.

Family plays a big part in the business. Brother Jamie is their talented Head Chef, whilst brother Mark manages their latest food and drink venture in Caxton – No.77 Thai Restaurant and Bar.

The Willow Tree is elegant, intimate and relaxed – well regarded as a charming venue for all seasons. An open fireplace awaits along with sparkling chandeliers, sumptuous shabby chic interiors and a candle-lit restaurant and bar.

The quirky outside areas include a dining terrace, a magical country garden boasting a giant willow with tree swings, and a huge tipi for special events and private dining.

Recommended by Michelin, AA, Alistair Sawdays and The Good Pub Guide, their creative, diverse and seasonal menu is lovingly created from fresh, local produce. Daily surprise specials are available via their 'Looking Glass' board. A hand-picked selection of wonderful world wines, local ales, international lagers and seasonal cocktails and mocktails will keep you well satiated. Regular events such as live jazz, outdoor theatre shows, burlesque nights, a summer ball and drinks festivals add to The Willow Tree's appeal. Alternatively, you can hold your own special event or wedding – where the affable team will work closely with you to make it an enchanting experience.

For independent and thoroughly innovative head to The Willow Tree and you'll dine happily ever after...

The Willow Tree
BALLOTINE OF PORK

Parma ham & cavolo nero, shallot purée, olive powder, fondant potato, seasonal vegetables
Lovely, locally sourced ingredients, combine to create a scrumptious fusion of flavours and
textures – delightful at any time of year. Serves 4.

Ingredients

For the pork ballotine:

500g pork fillet

300g cavolo nero

6 slices Parma ham

For the shallot purée:

5 large shallots

4 cloves garlic

Vegetable oil

Sprig of thyme

For the olive powder:

100g black olives

150g malto

For the fondant potatoes:

2 potatoes

300g butter

Sprig of rosemary and thyme

For the seasonal vegetables:

1 broccoli

100g peas

100g broad beans

2 shallots sliced

½ fennel bulb

Method

For the olive powder, finely dice the olives and bake at 60°c for 12 hours until dry. Add to blender with malto.

For the pork ballotine, firstly bring a pan of water to the boil, blanch your cavolo nero for two minutes until al dente and refresh in ice cold water. Drain any excess water. Prepare pork by removing any sinew then, in a hot frying pan, sear your meat. Add seasoning.

Lay out a sheet of cling film. Lay three slices of Parma ham vertically next to each other, add your cavolo nero, then pork – roll in to a cylinder and then tie off the ends. Cool in the fridge for 1 hour.

For the shallot purée, peel your shallots and garlic, add to ovenproof dish along with herbs and submerge with oil. Put tin foil on top and cook in the oven at 180°c for 3 hours.

Once cooked, drain oil, and add shallots to blender along with 100ml water. Blitz and season.

For the fondant potato, dice the potato, add to a small oven roasting tray and submerge potatoes in butter and herbs. Cook for 30 minutes at 200°c.

Once ready to serve, preheat oven to 220°c, boil a pan of water, poach ballotine for 7 minutes then remove cling film. Add to oven for 12 minutes along with your fondant potatoes.

Serve with your purée, powder and vegetables.

Here we have used the seasonal vegetables listed, however we recommend you talk to your local producers to find out what's in season locally, and therefore at its tastiest.

Baked to
PERFECTION

The winner of Cambridge Bake Off 2015, Jin Yee Chung gives us an insight into how he became a champion baker...

My baking influence comes, without doubt, from my mum. I grew up surrounded by cakes, cookies and bread, as she ran a home bakery taking orders for events and occasionally running baking classes. I never baked with her though – not even once – but I loved watching her in action. I think maybe that's how I picked up most of my baking techniques.

That was back in Malaysia, before I left to pursue further education in the UK, ultimately deciding to stay on for my professional career in Cambridge. Baking was always on my to-do list, but I never got round to it because of other priorities in life. I only started baking seriously after I bought myself a stand mixer at the Boxing Day sales in 2013. Since then, I set myself a challenge to at least bake something every fortnight – and I did! The more I bake, the more I love baking.

As a scientist, I like to 'experiment'... adding fusion touches and combining tastes from the Far East with Western styles. Baking allows me to combine my three passions – creativity, music (everything tastes better when it's made with music) and producing something which gives pleasure to other people.

Entering the Cambridge Bake Off 2015 was an incentive to push my baking skills further – and winning it has certainly boosted my confidence in the kitchen. Hearing the judges' unanimous decision on my showstopper, 'DNA cake', prompted me to seriously consider a career in baking. At the time of writing this, I still work as a scientist by day – but bake even more by night.

I hope this is just the beginning of something special!

Jin Yee Chung's
PANDAN LAYER CAKE

This cake is a light chiffon sponge, layered with a creamy coconut flavoured pandan-infused set custard. It's very popular in South East Asia because of its light texture and refreshing flavour. Due to the tropical climate there, it's best served chilled – and it's one of my favourite childhood desserts!

Ingredients

For the cake:

5 egg yolks

30g caster sugar

70ml water

50ml vegetable oil

80g self-raising flour

½ tsp baking powder

⅛ tsp salt

½ tsp pandan extract

5 egg whites

70g caster sugar

For the pandan coconut custard filling:

300ml coconut milk

800ml water

180g sugar

1½ tsp agar agar powder

80g custard powder

20g cornflour

½ tsp pandan extract

15g butter

Pinch of salt

For the garnish:

50g desiccated coconut

Fruits of your choice (optional)

Method

For the cake

Preheat oven to 160°c.

First prepare the egg yolks mixture. Beat egg yolks and 30g caster sugar until the sugar dissolves, then add in water, oil and pandan extract. Sift the flour, baking powder and salt. Mix until the mixture combines. Put aside.

In a separate mixing bowl, whisk egg whites until soft peaks, add 70g caster sugar while continuing to whisk until stiff peaks. Do not over beat the egg whites until too stiff as this will cause the cake to become too dry when baked. The meringue mixture is done.

Gently beat a third of the meringue into egg yolks mixture. Then fold in the remaining meringue until the mixture is well incorporated.

Pour the mixture into three 8" cake tins and bake for 45 minutes. Remove the cake from the oven. On a cooling rack, with the cake still in the tin, cool the cake upside down. When it has completely cooled down to room temperature, remove the cake from the tin. Now, prepare the filling.

For the pandan coconut custard filling

Mix all the ingredients except butter until everything is fully dissolved and form a smooth mixtures. Now pour this mixture into a pan, continue to stir on a medium heat until the mixture boils and thickens. Remove the mixture from the heat and stir in butter until dissolved.

Pass the mixture through a sieve to remove residual lumps, then cool slightly before pouring on to the chiffon cake sponge.

To assemble

Place one of the cakes in the bottom of an 8" cake ring and pour a third of the pandan coconut custard filling onto it. Wait for the filling to thicken slightly (about 30 seconds) before adding the next layer of cake. Repeat for the second and third layering.

Place the assembled cake in the refrigerator until the filling is set. Remove the set pandan layer cake from cake ring, garnish the sides with desiccated coconut and decorate with your favourite fruits on top.

Raising a
GLASS...

When it comes to vino, Cambridge Wine Merchants
are simply the toast of the town...

The brainchild of dynamic duo Hal Wilson and Brett Turner, Cambridge Wine Merchants was formed after the two friends met at Peterhouse Ball in 1990 and bonded over their mutual love of wine. Realising they both wanted to work in the trade, but not be in someone else's pocket, CWM was born in 1993 – and they haven't looked back since.

A multi award-winner, they landed Merchant of the Year at the International Wine Challenge (the world's biggest wine competition) and have three times been voted the UK's No. 1 Independent Drinks Retailer amongst many other accolades.

Originally starting with one shop on Mill Road in Cambridge, they now have four throughout the city, each one offering their own area of expertise and indivduality, whilst serving their local communities.

Nationally, they're now one of the biggest independent wine merchants in the country – who continue to expand and inspire.

Stating they're 'only as good as the last bottle we sold', the pair buy with love and dedication – and are always on the lookout for funky one-offs and proper wine made by proper people.

Their range is absolutely massive with over 1200 wines, over 800 spirits, including 400 whiskies, 100 gins, rums, vodkas, brandies and liquers of every colour and creed. They also stock local ales, cocktail ingredients and cigars.

In addition, their Bridge Street Wine Bar opened in 2013, just by Magdalene Bridge, and has been popular since.

Combining expert staff, honest advice and superb service – not to mention throwing a large dose of fun into the mix – Cambridge Wine Merchants are onto a real winner. And we'll drink to that...

Cambridge Wine Merchants

Recommended
WINE LIST

Our partners Cambridge Wine Merchants have recommended the following wines and beers so you can be sure to have the perfect accompaniment for each recipe in this book. They're all available at Cambridge Wine Merchants branches or online at www.cambridgewine.com.

Afternoon Tease: Orange drizzle cake with dark chocolate ganache
Ramos Pinto Quinta da Ervamoira 10yo Tawny £20 (50cl)

Orange and chocolate? Pass the Port! This aged tawny port has an orange citrusy side to it as well as the raisiny, chocolately, nutty flavours that are so moreish.

Aromi: Cartocciate spinaci – spinach calzoni
Negroamaro 'Terramare' 2013 IGT Salento, Feudi di Guagnano £7

This modestly priced red from the Negroamaro grape tastes anything but modest in the glass. A warm, sunny, brambly fruit, with slightly bitter chocolate tones and a velvety texture. It's great with Italian dishes especially this cartocciate, you'll be transported to Sicily in a heartbeat.

Blue Lion: Rabbit three ways – wellington, rabbit croquette and rabbit cottage pie
Robert Oatley Signature Pinot Noir 2013 Yarra Valley £14

The lovely varietal intensity in the wild strawberry, cherry and lightly savoury spectrum will pair wonderfully with the lean rabbit, whilst the vibrant and juicy nature of the grape will not overpower the dish. The gentle French oak influence will add wonderful background flavours.

Cambscuisine: Duck parcels, with sweet and sour cucumber
Dom. des Trinités Pech Mege 2013 Pezenas Rouge £12

Pech Mege is a silky, focused wine showing deep red fruits and the fresh minerality which is a characteristic of the schist soil of the Trinités vineyards. The mature fresh fruit will complement the sweet and sour aspect of the dish whilst the mellow spiced notes of the Grenache, Syrah and Carignan blend will suit the duck.

Cambridge Cookery School: Fresh asparagus, nectarine, avocado and crab salad
Lopez de Haro Rioja Blanco Barrica 2014 £8

Tine's gorgeous salad is perfectly complemented by this young white Rioja. Barrel fermented, and aged for 3 months, this has just the right amount of oak to make it unmistakeably Rioja, without letting the oak overpower the subtle fruit.

The Carpenters Arms: Scallops with puy lentils and a tomato and mixed herb sauce
Ch. St Pierre Tradition Provence Rosé 2014 £10

This dish is wonderfully tasty, comforting and southern French. And so is this wine! A big flavoured Rosé that is so elegantly pale pink, full of Provence character and a match for seafood, tomatoes and herbs. Yum!

The Carpenters Arms: Sablés Breton

Solera 1847 Oloroso Dulce Cream Sherry, Gonzalez Byass £13

These delicious crumbly buttery biscuits deserve an equally moreish wine match and we can't think better than the exquisitely drinkable Solera 1847 Cream Sherry: dark mahogany in colour, velvety soft on the palate conjuring flavours of dried figs and raisins, with a toffee finish.

Cheese+: Baked cheese

Esporao Reserva Branco 2013 Alentejo £12.50

Big flavoured cheese needs a big flavoured wine, but not necessarily red. This Portuguese white has huge personality, made by one of the great Australian winemakers David Bavistock. Plenty of rich fruit, showing tangerine, grapefruit and peach flavours backed up with subtle, spicy oak undertones.

Chequers of Orwell: Duo of duck with fondant potato, almond purée, broccoli and rhubarb

Fixin 'Les Crais' 2009 Dom. Denis Berthaut £28

Duck, bring the Pinot! This classic Burgundian has the best balance of pure ripe cherry fruit and delicate acidity. Juicy but supple tannins are what you want for the light gamey style of duck. The earthy potato and broccoli will be lifted by the light oak of the wine.

Chocolat Chocolat: Salted caramel truffles

Ch. du Cedre Malbec 2011 Vin de Liqueur 50cl £19

A close cousin of Vintage Porto, it has less alcohol and residual sugar (100 gr per litre). It presents a very fruity and complex nose of blackberry, cassis and hints of violet, spices and cocoa. Smooth and velvety on the palate, with a long finish.

Clare College: Vanilla confit salmon, crispy skin, lime emulsion, pickled vegetables

Riesling Grand Cru Schlossberg 2012 Cave de Kientzheim Kaysersberg £16

The hints of vanilla and buttery texture of the salmon are cut through by the steely yet rich style of this Grand Cru. The orange citrus notes will balance well with the lime emulsion and pickled vegetables.

Croxton Park: Pork ragu

La Chaussynette 2014 Mas du Boislauzon £11

Made up wholly of declassified Chateauneuf du Pape and Cotes du Rhone Villages fruit from the extremely highly regarded Mas de Boislauzon estate. The sweet, ripe and dark fruits will match perfectly with the flavoursome Oxford Sandy and Black pigs reared at Croxton Park. The full bodied and wholesome flavours will suit the classic character of a rich ragu.

Dale Pinnock: Chicken stuffed with spinach and sun-dried tomatoes with Mediterranean lentil stew

Montaignan Carignan Vieilles Vignes 2014, Southern France £7.50

Typically juicy, with lots of delicious red fruits, a lick of oak adding some vanilla, and soft tannins at the finish. Every mouthful is so enjoyable, as is the chicken.

Elder Street Farm Shop and Deli: Buffalo burgers

Tim Smith Wines Bugalugs Shiraz 2013 Barossa £15

Tim Smith is a highly decorated winemaker who has spent the last two decades making wine for some of Australia's most respected wineries. This is an easy drinking Barossa Shiraz that's packed with vibrant, upfront fruit, and a really great balance of acidity and tannins. The perfect match for a succulent Buffalo burger, it will only add to the sweet and tender nature of Buffalo meat.

The Free Press: Black pudding Scotch egg with a smoky tomato chutney

Harviestoun Brewery Old Engine Oil Porter 6.0% 33cl £2

Smooth, creamy brew with a beautiful velvety mouthfeel. Enjoy flavours of coffee, slightly buttered toffee, dark chocolate and earthy hops. You may find some mild cherry fruit within the residual sweetness, neatly accompanying roasted flavours.

George Hotel: Roasted fillet of wild sea bass with Israeli couscous, brown shrimps, clams, peas, broad beans and lemon butter sauce

Santenay Blanc Sous La Roche 2013 Bachey-Legros £20

Outstanding Santenay Blanc from the growers with the oldest vines in the appellation. Ideal for the roasted sea bass, its delicate sweet flavours suit the subtle smoky character of the oak yet there remains enough mineral and citrus character for the lemon butter sauce and shellfish.

Gog Magog Hills: Coolea and garlic mushroom tartlet
Vondeling Babiana 2012 South Africa £14

An outstanding blend of Chenin Blanc, Chardonnay, Viognier and Grenache blanc. The classic Coolea flavours of hazelnut, butterScotch and honey pair beautifully with the honeydew, baked quince and rich texture of the Babiana. Possibly the perfect pairing for Gog Magog Hill sundowners.

Inder's Kitchen: Keralan chicken curry
Wiper And True No.10 Small Beer 2.6% 33cl £2.30

Inder's cuisine is subtle and delicious and I've enjoyed many a good bottle of wine with it, but here's a great opportunity to expand your beer horizons with some wonderful food. Wiper and True are a sensational Bristol brewery and their special edition Small Beer has wonderful citrusy hops that will go beautifully with the Keralan curry. Lower alcohol too, but no shortage on flavour.

Jack's Gelato: Rhubarb sorbet
Moscato Frizzante Piemonte Volpi 5.5% £10

Late-picked naturally sweet Moscato (Muscat) grapes produce this irresistible fizz. A smell like a bag of sultanas leads on to sweet baked-apple fruit. The sweet and fruity style of this wine allows the slightly tart yet fresh rhubarb to dance across the palate with the delicate sorbet mouth feel.

Jin Yee Chung: Pandan cake with coconut filling
Muscat de Rivesaltes 2012 Domaine Treloar, Roussillon, France £12 (50cl)

Rich, opulent, thick and beautifully scented. Really clean and fresh – none of the harshness and fire that you can get with this style. Sophisticated and perfect with this delicious cake.

The Larder at Burwash Manor: Pork tenderloin and asparagus baked in pastry
Vouvray Sec Tendre 2013 Ch. Gaudrelle £14

A great match for pork is apple; well this Chenin blanc has all the flavours of apple, quince and fig. Rounded, full-bodied and acidulous apple and honey with an off-dry finish ideal for the buttery flaky pastry.

Midsummer House: Asparagus with potato cannelloni, hollandaise, white wine shallot rings and burnt onion powder
Ch. Latour Martillac Pessac Leognan Blanc 2012 £36

This classic Bordeaux Blanc has delightful citrus marmalade, mango and tropical fruit notes along with subtle hints of crème brûlée. The buttery, tart hollandaise and the green, vegetal style of fresh asparagus are complemented by the zesty and fresh Sauvignon while the influence of oak has enough richness to play with the potato cannelloni and burnt onion powder.

The Merry Monk: Jacobs ladder beef short ribs
Pertaringa Understudy Cabernet Sauvignon 2013 McLaren Vale £15

What better than an inky, New World Cabernet to accompany these sticky ribs? Pertaringa winemaker Shane Harris makes a superb McLaren Vale Cab, with intensely concentrated flavours but bright acid and chewy tannins. Dig in!

Nanna Mexico: Chiles en nogada
Los Espinos Merlot 2014 Central Valley £7

The diurnal range in Chile's Central Valley ensures the grapes ripen slowly, so they develop maximum flavour. The soft super-juicy ripe plummy fruit served up by this great value Merlot really suits the succulent chicken or beef wrapped in Poblano Chilli and the long full-flavoured finish pairs wonderfully with the walnut cream.

Norfolk Street: Blueberry cake
Ch. La Haute Borie 2010 Monbazillac £12

With a moist cake you need something equally sweet but with refreshing acidity. This Monbazillac wine is wonderfully sweet, soft and well rounded with hints of lemon and tangerine. A perfect accompaniment.

The Offord Shoe: Chargrilled tuna with chilli, garlic and oregano in borlotti bean and roasted red pepper stew and courgette ribbons
Biferno Palladino Rosso Riserva DOC 2009 Camillo de Lellis, Molise £9

This wine comes from the Achilles heel area of Italy, a little known region called Molise that makes savoury, age worthy wines which are the perfect accompaniment to spicy Mediterranean dishes like this one.

The OOO Company: That chicken and olive thing

Dom. La Combe Blanche L'Incompris Cinsault Rouge 2013 IGP Cotes du Brian £9

Blackcurrants on the nose with garrigue (Southern French scrubland smell!) and peppery, spicy notes. Very upfront, enticing fruit flavours – brambles and raspberries. Smooth, rounded tannins and an appealing freshness. Gorgeous with chicken.

The Pantry: Pig's head terrine

Humbleyard Bacchus Dry White 2013 England £13

An East Anglian wine made from the Bacchus grape and really delicious. A great match with the terrine, it has bright acidity, elderflower and citrusy flavours.

Pint Shop: Lamb, peas and bread

Rosso del Palazzone Lotto 2014/01 Il Palazzone £14

Lamb requires big flavours as well as good acidity, which leads us to Italy and this 'baby' Brunello di Montalcino from Il Palazzone. It has all the deep cherry, herbs and savoury power of the best sangiovese from the area. Real Brunello character at a fraction of the price.

Red Lion/Black Bull: Poppy seed crusted fillet of venison

Ch. Bernadotte 2008 Haut Medoc Cru Bourgeois £15

There are so many deer in South West France that matching the great wines of Bordeaux with venison is a no brainer. This one comes from a vineyard next to Pauillac and was made by one of its most famous chateaux, Ch. Pichon Longueville, Comtesse de Lalande.

Sedgwick's Charcuterie: Chicken with rare breed sobrassada and cannellini beans

Dom. Danjou-Banessy Les Myrs Rouge 2013 Cotes du Roussillon Villages £30

A beautifully lifted, fragant and bright nose. This 80yr old vine Carignan has minerality and fruit capable of pairing with the paprika and spices of the sobrassada. It has the charm of a top quality Burgundy.

Shelford Deli: Rhubarb, orange and almond polenta cake

Coteaux du Layon Tri de Vendange 2011 Dom. du Landreau £19

Harvested at three points in the vintage, the result is a luscious, rich mouth feel without being overly sweet and cloying. The orange and almond flavours will be balanced by the almost baked quince notes, while the bright rhubarb will be leave you wanting more of the golden wine.

Shelford Deli: Slow roast lamb with Manzanilla sherry and spinach

Lopez de Haro Rioja Crianza 2012 £9

Classical in its style, lightly-colored, with clean red spicy fruit, a touch of leather and a polished, soft palate that makes it a very good pairing for slow-roasted lamb. The savoury edge will complement the salty Manzanilla and nutty spinach.

Tom's Cakes: Ginger cake

Bacalhoa Moscatel de Setubal 2012 £11

This is ginger cake in a glass! Intense moscatel aromas of orange flower, ginger, tea and raisins. Intense, very sweet, sticky and full-bodied wine, with sweet and sour sensations, and a long and persistent finish.

The White Pheasant: Beetroot mousse, pine nuts, whipped goats' cheese, pear and pickles

Sancerre Blanc 2014 Dom. Noel et Jean-Luc Raimbault £15

All of these ingredients suggest Sauvignon Blanc as a pairing, particularly the goats' cheese which leads us to the Loire Valley and Sancerre in particular, where the locals are equally at home making wine or raising goats' for cheese.

The Willow Tree: Ballotine of pork, Parma ham and cavolo nero with shallot purée, olive powder, fondant potato and seasonal vegetables

Valpolicella Ripasso Superiore DOC Ripasso 'Bosan' 2011 Cesari £20

Those great Italian ingredients need a seriously good Italian wine and in the single vineyard Bosan Valpolicella we have a worthy partner. It's a full-flavoured Ripasso with a sweet and sour push-pull of dark fruit flavours intermingled with an attractive spicy bitterness and soft tannins with a touch of sweetness.
A long, velvety, dried fruit and sweet spice finish seals the deal. Foodie heaven!

NEWZEALAND

AUSTRALIA

The DIRECTORY

These great businesses have supported the making of this book; please support and enjoy them.

Afternoon Tease
13 King St,
Cambridge, CB1 1LH
Website: www.afternoontease.co.uk
Independent café serving breakfast, brunch, lunch and an ever-changing selection of homemade cakes.

The Anchor Inn
Bury Lane, Sutton Gault,
Ely, CB6 2BD
Telephone: 01353 778537
Website:
www.anchor-inn-restaurant.co.uk
Award-winning Fenland restaurant with letting rooms.

Aromi
1 Bene't Street,
Cambridge, CB2 3QN
Telephone: 01223 300117
Website: www.aromi.co.uk
An independent café, based in the heart of Cambridge, offering freshly prepared and authentic Italian food with a Sicilian twist.

Barker Bros Butchers
43 High Street, Great Shelford,
Cambridge, CB22 5EH
Telephone: 01223 843292
Website:
www.barkerbrosbutchers.co.uk
Trading since 1843, Barker Bros is a traditional family run butchers shop nestled in the picturesque village of Great Shelford.

The Black Bull Inn
27 High Street, Balsham,
Cambridge, CB21 4DJ
Telephone: 01223 893 844
Website: www.blackbull-balsham.co.uk
An independent thatched country inn and restaurant with five set apart guest accommodation rooms in a quiet rural conservation village.

The Blue Lion
74 Main Street, Hardwick,
Cambridge, CB23 7QU
Telephone: 01954 210328
Website: www.bluelionhardwick.co.uk
Picturesque gastropub serving freshly prepared seasonal and innovative food with impeccable service.

Cambridge Chop House
1 King's Parade,
Cambridge, CB2 1SJ
Telephone: 01223 359506
Website: www.cambscuisine.com
The Cambridge Chop House is an upscale rustic restaurant with an old-school British menu, set in a vaulted cellar dining room.

Cambridge Cookery School
School House, Homerton Gardens,
Purbeck Road, CB2 8EB
Telephone: 01223 247620
Website:
www.cambridgecookeryschool.com
Award-winning cookery school in the beautiful city of Cambridge.

Cambridge Dining Company
Button End, Harston,
Cambridge, CB22 7GX
Telephone: 01223 874333
Website: www.cambridgedining.co.uk
Part of the Cambscuisine group, and a specialist event planning service.

The Cambridge Distillery
By appointment only.
Telephone: 01223 269209
Website:
www.cambridgedistillery.co.uk
The world's first gin tailor.

Cambridge Food Tour
Telephone: 01223 269991
Website: www.cambridgefoodtour.com
Walking food tours taking you off the beaten path and showing the best of the British and Cambridge food scene through the eyes of a foodie, spiced with local tales and history.

Cambridge Wine Merchants
32 Bridge St, City Centre,
Cambridge, CB2 1UJ
Telephone: 01223 568989
Website: www.cambridgewine.com
Independent merchants offering wines, beers and spirits plus an on-site wine bar and wine-tasting events.

The Carpenters Arms
10 High St,
Great Wilbraham,
Cambridge, CB21 5JD
Telephone: 01223 882093
Website:
www.carpentersarmsgastropub.co.uk
White-painted village pub offering both classic French cuisine and real ales in a cosy ambiance.

The Cock (Cambscuisine)
47 High Street,
Hemingford Grey, PE28 9BJ
Telephone: 01480 463609
Website: www.cambscuisine.com
One of group of six local restaurants and event catering operation based in Cambridgeshire. The Cock is a pub and restaurant serving fresh, seasonal food.

Cheese+
64 Papworth Business Park,
Atria Court, Stirling Way,
Papworth Everard,
Cambridge, CB23 3GY
Telephone: 01480 831112
Website: www.cheese-plus.co.uk
Cheese+ is a specialist cheese company supplying the finest artisan cheese, charcuterie, and olives – plus everything else you would expect to find in your favourite delicatessen.

The Chequers
22 Town Green Road,
Orwell, SG8 5QL
Telephone: 01223 207840
Website:
www.thechequersoforwell.co.uk
Cosy gastropub with an open fire in winter and an outside area, serving steaks, grills and salads.

Chocolat Chocolat
21 St Andrews Street,
Grand Arcade,
Cambridge, CB2 3AX
Telephone: 01223 778982
Website: www.chocolatchocolat.co.uk
Independent chocolatiers, famous for delicious handmade sheet chocolate, made with the finest Belgian chocolate in a unique French style, as well as a range of confectionary, ice cream in the summer and hot chocolate in the winter.

Clare College Catering
Old Court, Trinity Lane,
Cambridge, CB2 1TL
Telephone: 01223 333227
Website: www.clareconferencing.com
The Clare College catering department is manned by staff from diverse backgrounds – creating a harmonious and positive blend in the delivery of its services.

Croxton Park Partnership
Croxton Park,
St. Neots, PE19 6SY
Telephone: 01480 880345
Website: www.croxtonpark.eu
Organic mixed farm in Cambridgeshire with pedigree beef shorthorn herd.

Elder Street Café and Deli
Debden Barns,
Elder Street, Debden,
Saffron Walden, CB11 3JY
Telephone: 01799 544 018
Website: www.elderstreetcafedeli.co.uk
Purveyors of homemade and locally sourced speciality foods.

The Free Press
7 Prospect Row,
Cambridge, CB1 1DU
Telephone: 01223 368337
Website: www.freepresspub.com
Traditional pub serving real ale and home cooked food.

The George Hotel and Brasserie
High Street, Buckden,
St Neots, PE19 5XA
Telephone: 01480 812300
Website: www.thegeorgebuckden.com
Small boutique hotel, wine bar and brasserie. Bringing a little bit of London styling to the heart of Cambridgeshire.

Gog Magog Hills
Heath Farm, Shelford Bottom,
Cambridge, CB22 3AD
Telephone: 01223 248 352
Website: gogmagoghills.com
A busy, family-owned farm shop, deli, café and award-winning butchery in Cambridge.

The Horseshoe Inn
90 High Street,
Offord Darcy, PE19 5RH
Telephone: 01480 810293
Website: www.theoffordshoe.co.uk
Family run, award-winning dining pub,
in the picturesque village of Offord Darcy.

Inder's Kitchen Ltd
43 Clifton Road,
Cambridge, CB1 7ED
Telephone: 01223 211333
Website: www.inderskitchen.com
Serving the residents of Cambridge with
true Indian cooking since 2010.

Jack's Gelato
5-7 Sussex Street,
Cambridge, CB1 1PA
Telephone: 07909 224178
Website: jacksgelato.co.uk
Expertly crafted ice creams and sorbets.

The Larder
Burwash Manor,
New Road, Barton,
Cambridge, CB23 7EY
Telephone: 01223 264600
Website: www.burwashlarder.com
The Larder at Burwash Manor is a farm
shop on the outskirts of Cambridge, selling
organic asparagus and rare breed pork
from the working farm.

The Merry Monk
30 West Street, Isleham,
Ely, CB7 5SB
Telephone: 01638 8780900
Website: www.merry-monk.co.uk
Inspired, relaxed dishes, with fresh
flavours.

Midsummer House
Midsummer Common,
Cambridge, CB4 1HA
Telephone: 01223 369299
Website: www.midsummerhouse.co.uk
Two Michelin starred Victorian-era,
riverside cottage serving elegant French
meals at smart tables in a dining
conservatory.

Nanna Mexico
33 Regent Terrace,
Cambridge, CB2 1AB
Telephone: 07854 617603
Website: www.nannamexico.com
Relaxed, modern restaurant serving fresh
and authentic Mexican classics.

Norfolk Street Bakery
89 Norfolk Street,
Cambridge, CB1 2LD
Telephone: 01223 660 163
Website: www.norfolkstreetbakery.com
Artisan bakery serving a delicious
selection of British and Portuguese breads
and pastries.

The OOO Company
Olive Tree Cottage,
School Road, Broughton,
Huntingdon, PE28 3AT
Telephone: 07824387933
Website: www.ooocompany.com
Producers of 100% extra virgin olive oil,
flavoured olive oil, flavoured olives and
village style halloumi cheese direct from
the makers in Cyprus.

The Pantry
Unit 17 and 18,
The Guineas, Newmarket,
CB8 8EQ
Telephone: 01638 661181
Website: www.thepantryfinefoods.com
Fine food shop and restaurant –
showcasing the best the region has to offer.

Pint Shop
10 Peas Hill,
Cambridge, CB2 3PN
Telephone: 01223 352293
Website: www.pintshop.co.uk
Meat. bread. beer.

The Prince Albert
62 Silver Street,
Ely, CB7 4JF
Telephone: 01353 663494
Traditional backstreet pub with ten real
ale hand pumps, stylish dining room and
large garden.

The Red Lion Inn
32 High St,
Hinxton, Cambridge
CB10 1QY
Telephone: 01799 530 601
Website: www.redlionhinxton.co.uk
An independent country inn and
restaurant with eight mews style
guest accommodation rooms in a quiet
conservation village.

The Royal Standard
24 Forehill,
Ely, CB7 4AF
Telephone: 01353 645194
Website: www.theroyalstandardely.com
Steak and seafood restaurant with great
cocktails and an eclectic wine list.

Sedgwick's Charcuterie
1 and 2 The Green,
High Street,
Toseland, PE19 6RX
Telephone: 01480 880165
Website: sedgwickscharcuterie.co.uk
Artisan cured meats from Sedgwick's
smallholding.

Shelford Delicatessen
8a Woollards Lane,
Great Shelford, Cambridge,
CB22 5LZ
Telephone: 01223 846129
Website: www.shelforddeli.co.uk
*Artisan kitchen, delicatessen and café
creating wholesome food to eat in, take out
or order for an event.*

Smokeworks
2 Free School Ln,
Cambridge, CB2 3QA
Website: www.smokeworks.co.uk
*Smoked, pulled, brined and seasoned
classic barbecue food paired with beer,
bourbon and milkshakes. Delivered fast,
eat–in or take-out.*

St John's Chop House
21-24 Northampton St,
Cambridge, CB3 0AD
Telephone: 01223 353110
Website: www.cambscuisine.com
*19th-century brick eatery with wood-
burning stoves and exposed beams,
serving meaty British cuisine.*

Tickell Arms
1 North Rd, Whittlesford,
Cambridge, CB22 4NZ
Telephone: 01223 833025
Website: www.cambscuisine.com
*Village pub with a smart, modern
conservatory dining room, large fireplace
and bowler hats as lamps.*

Tom's Cakes Ltd
19 Market Hill,
St Ives, PE27 5AL
Telephone: 01487 842200
Website: www.tomscakes.co.uk
*Truly scrumptious handmade cakes and
biscuits, available to take away or enjoy
in the unique café with a delicious cup of
Monmouth coffee, or a pot of Kandula
Tea.*

The Urban Shed
62-64 King Street,
Cambridge, CB1 1LN
Telephone: 01223 324888
Website: www.theurbanshed.com
Retro sandwich bar and coffee shop.

The White Pheasant
21 Market Street,
Fordham,
Ely, CB7 5LQ
Telephone: 01638 720414
Website: www.whitepheasant.com
*Creative contemporary dishes using
locally sourced produce in a smart country
restaurant and bar.*

The Willow Tree
29 High Street,
Bourn, CB23 2SQ
Telephone: 01954 719775
Website: www.thewillowtreebourn.com
Charming country gastropub.